The Music Teacher's
Almanac

Ready-to-Use Music Activities for Every Month of the Year

Loretta Mitchell

PARKER PUBLISHING COMPANY
West Nyack, New York 10995

*Several of the illustrations are reproductions from
Dover Publications, Inc.*

The author gratefully acknowledges the
contributions of Joanne Comstock, Jeff DeVaney,
Jane Frazee, and Gloria Kiester.

Library of Congress Cataloging-in-Publication Data

Mitchell, Loretta, 1951-
    The music teacher's almanac: ready-to-use music activities for every month of the year / Loretta Mitchell.
      p. cm.
    Includes indexes.
    ISBN 0-13-605601-6
    1. School music--Instruction and study--Activity programs.
  I. Title.
MT10.M6658 1992   91-42296
372.87´044--dc20   CIP
                                                             MN

ISBN 0-13-605601-6

 **Parker Publishing Company**
Professional Publishing
Englewood Cliffs, NJ 07632
Simon & Schuster. A Paramount Communications Company

Printed in the United States of America

ABOUT THE AUTHOR

LORETTA MITCHELL teaches elementary general and choral music for the Brainerd, Minnesota, Public Schools and serves as the school district 1–12 music coordinator. She has taught vocal, instrumental, and general music since 1973. A Phi Beta Kappa and summa cum laude graduate of St. Olaf College, she toured with both the St. Olaf Band and the St. Olaf Choir. She earned the master of science degree in music education from the University of Illinois at Urbana-Champaign.

Ms. Mitchell's professional awards include a graduate fellowship at the University of Illinois, Minnesota Professional Development Plan Fellowship, Brainerd Teacher of the Year, Minnesota Teacher of Excellence, Minnesota Honor Roll Teacher, and Minnesota Classroom Music Educator of the Year. She has presented workshops and clinics for state music education conferences, administrators, and classroom teachers across the Upper Midwest. She has held the offices of vice president and president of Minnesota Elementary Music Educators K–8 and classroom music vice president of Minnesota Music Educators Association. She has served on the Commissioner's Task Force for Restructuring Education, the Minnesota Department of Education Elementary Curriculum Rules Change Committee, and the Minnesota Model Learner Outcome Committee.

Other professional resources by Ms. Mitchell include *Music Reading Made Simple; One, Two, Three ... Echo Me!; 101 Bulletin Boards for the Music Classroom;* and the *Ready-to-Use Music Reading Activities Kit*. She is also a contributing author to *The Primary Teacher's Ready-to-Use Activities Program*.

ACKNOWLEDGEMENTS AND CREDITS

Grateful acknowledgement is extended to composers, publishers, and agents for permission to reprint the following. Intensive efforts have been made to locate all copyright owners. Any omissions or errors were inadvertent, and will be corrected upon reprint.

LET'S GO FLY A KITE
Words and Music by
Richard M. Sherman and Robert B. Sherman
© 1963 Wonderland Music Company Inc.
Copyright renewed
Used by permission

THE STARS AND STRIPES FOREVER
Listening map adapted from original map by Gloria Kiester
St. Olaf College, Northfield, MN 55057
Used by permission

UNSQUARE DANCE
by Dave Brubeck
© 1962, renewed 1990, Derry Music Company
601 Montgomery St. Suite 800, San Francisco, CA 94111
Used by permission

RHAPSODY IN BLUE
(George Gershwin)
© 1924 WB MUSIC CORP. (Renewed)
All Rights Reserved.
Used by permission

LITTLE ORPHANT ANNIE
Adapted from "Little Orphant Annie" from THE COMPLETE WORKS OF JAMES WHITCOMB RILEY, Vol. 3, edited by Edmund Henry Eitel (Indianapolis, Bobbs-Merrill, 1913)

THIS LAND IS YOUR LAND
Words and Music by Woody Guthrie
TRO — © Copyright 1956 (renewed) 1958 (renewed) and 1970
Ludlow Music, Inc., New York, NY
Used by permission
Instrumental accompaniments by Jane Frazee,
Director, University of St. Thomas Institute
for Contemporary Music Education. Used by permission

BLACK AND GOLD
© Melvin Lee Steadman, Jr.
Falls Church, VA 22046

THANK YOU, LORD
© Loretta Mitchell
Instrumental accompaniments by Jane Frazee,
Director, University of St. Thomas Institute
for Contemporary Music Education. Used by permission

CANOE SONG
Instrumental accompaniments by Jane Frazee,
Director, University of St. Thomas Institute
for Contemporary Music Education. Used by permission

ABOUT THIS ALMANAC

The Music Teacher's Almanac provides ready-to-use music activities to supplement and extend the music curriculum. The activities teach fundamental music skills and concepts while they commemorate special events, seasons, and holidays of the calendar year. This kit will be a valuable resource for music specialists and classroom teachers of grades K–8.

The Music Teacher's Almanac has the following unique features:

• Activities are based on musical experiences. Unlike books full of reproducible music theory worksheets, these activities go far beyond the pencil-and-paper approach. Each activity begins and ends with music and involves the student in a musical context, leading to musical learning.

• Musical examples include classical works and folk songs as well as original compositions.

• Activities reinforce basic concepts in the elements of music: melody, harmony, form, rhythm, timbre, and expression.

• Activities reinforce a variety of music skills: singing, playing, moving, listening, analyzing, composing, reading, and writing music.

• This book includes several time-saving devices for the teacher:

—Activities are sequenced according to the months of the year.

—Activities outline suggested grade level(s), objective, materials, preparation suggestions, directions, and answer keys.

—Activities are ready to use and can be duplicated in any quantity needed.

—Activities are extensively indexed by alphabet, subject, concept, skill, and suggested grade level.

• Activities use the most basic equipment, recorded musical examples, and materials. Use of this almanac does not require additional purchases.

• Activities are designed to challenge students' higher-order thinking skills. You will notice, for example, the many composition projects and use of upper taxonomy-level questions throughout the book.

• Activities include a variety of cultures, are gender-fair, and are disability-sensitive.

• Activities can be easily adapted for a wide range of student abilities and for students with special needs.

Using the natural motivation of seasons, holidays, and special events, the learning activities included for each month are educationally sound, conceptually balanced, and musically valid. For example,

—SEPTEMBER includes a composition project for Grandparent's Day, a listening map for George Gershwin's birthday, and an instrumental accompaniment for Native American Day.

—OCTOBER features a pitch matching game for Columbus Day, a research project for United Nations Day, a speech rondo and partner songs for Halloween, and an improvised opera for the birthday of the Metropolitan Opera House.

—NOVEMBER includes the Aaron Copland Hall of Fame, a listening map for Sousa's "Sempre Fidelis," a Thanksgiving round with Orff-style accompaniment, and a research project to celebrate American Music Week.

—In DECEMBER, musical icons and symbolic notation are included in an activity for Hanukkah. Christmas activities range from the creation of a theme and variations to a dramatization of the Nutcracker story. Listening activities are included for such classics as the "Hallelujah Chorus" and Beethoven's Fifth Symphony.

—In JANUARY, Martin Luther King Day provides motivation for student improvisation, culminating in the rondo "Martin." January also includes chord building for the New Year, a trivia research project, and analysis of Mozart's Symphony No. 40.

—FEBRUARY includes a rhythm game and a form activity for Valentine's Day, transposing a Groundhog Day song, and analysis of Chopin's "The Minute Waltz."

—MARCH offers a writing activity for Music in Our Schools Month, and a dramatization and sequencing activity for National Anthem Day.

—APRIL celebrates Easter with a melodic dictation activity, and includes a "Peter and the Wolf" listening activity, a finger play for springtime, an accompanied choral reading for Arbor Day, and "Twinkle, Twinkle, Little Star" in four-part barbershop style harmony!

—MAY activities include a call-and-response performance for Jewish Heritage Week, a composition project for Mother's Day, three listening maps for Carnival of the Animals, and a listening map for "The Stars and Stripes Forever."

—JUNE, JULY and AUGUST include a research project about Louis Armstrong, an opportunity for students to discover similarities in impressionistic painting and impressionistic music, a conducting activity for National Clown Week, an introduction to the sitar from India, and a rhythm band accompaniment for a baseball chant.

Students' excitement with seasons, holidays, and special events is a natural motivator for learning. *The Music Teacher's Almanac* puts a wealth of music learning activities, designed to capitalize on that natural motivation at your fingertips. Because these activities begin and end with music itself, they help students to maximize their natural musical potential, love of music, and love of musical learning.

My best wishes to you and your students for many wonderful musical learning experiences!

Loretta Mitchell

CONTENTS

About This Almanac / iv

SEPTEMBER
page 1

Grandmas (Grandpas) Are Like That / 1–1, 1–2
Composition Project / Grandparent's Day, Second Sunday of September

Sing of Peace / 1–3, 1–4
Round with Accompaniment / International Day of Peace, September 15

Admission: One Ticket / 1–5
Classroom Management / Back to School

Give a Cheer! / 1–6
Music Writing Activity / Football Season

Sounds of Autumn / 1–7
Sound Piece

Counting Acorns / 1–8
Pitch Matching Game

Rhapsody in Blue / 1–9
Listening Map / George Gershwin, September 26

Canoe Song / 1–10
Round / Native American Day, Fourth Friday in September

Canoe Song / 1–11
Vocal/Instrumental Activity / Native American Day, Fourth Friday in September

Names and Faces / 1–12
Rhythmic Chant / Back to School

Raking Leaves / 1–13
Rhythmic Chant

OCTOBER
page 21

Bushels of Apples / 2–1
Composition Project / National Apple Month

Popping, Popping / 2–2
Composition Project / National Popcorn Poppin' Month

Christopher Columbus / 2–3
Composition Project / Columbus Day, October 12

Who Stowed Away? / 2–4, 2–5
Pitch Matching Game / Columbus Day, October 12

Three Billy Goats Gruff / 2–6
Children's Opera / Opening of the Metropolitan Opera House, October 22, 1883

Songs from Around the World / 2–7, 2–8
Research Project / United Nations Day, October 24

Ten Little Costumes / 2–9
Rhythm Game / Halloween, October 31

Little Orphant Annie / 2–10, 2–11
Choral Reading / Halloween, October 31

Nine Lives / 2–12, 2–13
Reading and Performing Activity / Halloween, October 31

Black and Gold / 2–14, 2–15
Song with Accompaniment / Halloween, October 31

Trick or Treat / 2–16
Partner Song / Halloween, October 31

Caught in a Spider Web / 2–17, 2–18, 2–19
Note Name Game / Halloween, October 31

Halloween Rondo / 2–20 2–21
Speech Activity / Halloween, October 31

NOVEMBER
page 53

Extra! Extra! Our School Is Great! / 3–1
Speech Composition / American Education Week

American Composers / 3–2
Research Project / American Music Week

Sandwich Music / 3–3
  Listening Activity / *Sandwich Day, November 3*

Saxophones and Their Cousins / 3–4
  Listening Game / *Saxophone Day, November 6*

Sempre Fidelis / 3–5, 3–6
  Listening Map / *John Philip Sousa, November 6*

Aaron Copland Hall of Fame / 3–7
  Class Project / *Aaron Copland, November 14*

Young Person's Guide to the Orchestra / 3–8
  Listening Activity / *Benjamin Britten, November 22*

Maple Leaf Rag / 3–9
  Listening Map / *Scott Joplin, November 24*

On the First Thanksgiving / 3–10
  Composition Project / *Thanksgiving*

Thank You, Lord / 3–11
  Round with Accompaniment / *Thanksgiving*

Over the River and through the Wood / 3–12
  Musical Map / *Thanksgiving*

Turkey Shoot / 3–13
  Rhythmic Chant / *Thanksgiving*

DECEMBER
page 73

Unsquare Dance / 4–1
  Listening Guide / *Dave Brubeck, December 5*

Symphony No. 5 / 4–2
  Listening Activity / *Ludwig van Beethoven, December 16*

Dot Dot Dot Dash / 4–3
  Composition Project / *Ludwig van Beethoven, December 16*

Hanukkah / 4–4
  Sequencing Activity / *Hanukkah*

Violins and How They Work / 4–5
  Study Guide / *Antonio Stradivari, December 18*

Build Your Own String Instrument / 4–6
  Student Project / *Antonio Stradivari, December 18*

Holiday Rhythms / 4–7
    Rhythm Dictation | Hanukkah, Christmas

Christmas Carol Challenge / 4–8
    Listening Game

Jingle Bells / 4–9, 4–10
    Form Activity

Hallelujah Chrous / 4–11
    Listening Activity

Variations on a Familiar Carol / 4–12
    Creative Activity

The Story of the Nutcracker / 4–13
    Dramatization

JANUARY
page 95

A Song for the New Year / 5–1
    Composition Project | The New Year

New Year's Chords / 5–2
    Accompaniment Activity | The New Year

Music Trivia / 5–3
    Reseach Project | Trivia Day, January 4

Contrasts / 5–4
    Listening Guide | Elvis Presley, January 8

Martin / 5–5
    Rondo | Martin Luther King Day, Third Monday of January

Pizza for All / 5–6
    Speech Canon | National Pizza Week

Figure Eight Forms / 5–7
    Study Guide | Winter

Symphony No. 40 / 5–8
    Listening Guide | Wolfgang Amadeus Mozart, January 27

Doo Dah, Doo Dah / 5–9
    Sequencing Activity | Stephen Foster Memorial Day, January 13

The Trout / 5–10, 5–11
  Listening Guide / Franz Schubert, January 31

Gunpowder Run / 5–12, 5–13
  Music Theory Game

FEBRUARY
page 115

Take Care of Your Grin / 6–1
  Composition Project / Dental Health Month

Will We Have More Winter? / 6–2
  Transposing Project / Groundhog Day, February 2

Invent a Musical Instrument / 6–3
  Student Project / National Inventors Day, February 11

Love to Me, Love to You / 6–4, 6–5
  Rhythm Game / Valentine's Day, February 14

Love Somebody / 6–6
  Music Reading Activity: Icons / Valentine's Day, February 14

Love Somebody / 6–7
  Music Reading Activity: Symbolic Notation / Valentine's Day, February 14

Lovely Rhythms / 6–8
  Rhythm Dictation / Valentine's Day, February 14

The Minute Waltz / 6–9
  Listening Guide / Frederic Chopin, February 22

William Tell Overture / 6–10
  Listening Map / Giacchino Rossini, February 29

February Melodies / 6–11
  Melodic Dictation / Presidents' Day, Third Monday in February

MARCH
page 133

Celebrate Music Education / 7–1
  Creative Writing Project / Music in Our Schools Month

Peanuts Peanuts Peanuts / 7–2
  Rhythmic Chant / National Peanut Month

The Swing Era / 7–3
Listening Guide / Glenn Miller, March 1

O'er the Ramparts / 7–4
Dramatization / National Anthem Day, March 3

A Star-Spangled Melody / 7–5
Sequencing Activity / National Anthem Day, March 3

Hello, How Are You? / 7–6
Improvisation Activity / Anniversary of the Telephone, March 10

Johnny Appleseed / 7–7
Form Activity / Johnny Appleseed Day, March 11

Paddy Works on the Railway / 7–8
Composition Project / St. Patrick's Day, March 17

Little Fugue in G Minor / 7–9
Listening Map / J. S. Bach, March, 21

Happy Birthday, Dear Sebastian / 7–10, 7–11
Class Project / J. S. Bach, March 21

Surprise Symphony / 7–12
Listening Guide / Franz Joseph Haydn, March 31

Lions and Lambs / 7–13
Study Guide

Let's Go Fly a Kite / 7–14
Movement Plan

Windy Days of March / 7–15
Sound Piece

APRIL
page 157

April Fool / 8–1, 8–2
Composition Activity / April Fools' Day, April 1

They Call It Barbershop / 8–3
Four-Part Harmony / Barbershop Quartet Day, April 11

I Love to Read / 8–4
Composition Project / National Library Week

It's Time to Turn to Spring / 8–5
Finger Play

What Do We Plant When We Plant the Tree? / 8–6
Choral Reading with Accompaniment / Arbor Day

Peter and the Wolf / 8–7, 8–8
Listening activity / Sergei Prokofiev, April 23

Easter Egg Hunt / 8–9, 8–10
Melodic Dictation

Welcome Springtime / 8–11
Rhythm Sequencing Activity

It's Raining / 8–12
Harmony Activity

May
page 175

May Baskets / 9–1
Melodic Dictation / May Day, May 1

A Tisket, A Tasket / 9–2
Music Reading Activity / May Day, May 1

Long-Eared Personages / 9–3
Listening Map / Be Kind to Animals Week

Royal March of the Lion / 9–4
Listening Map / Be Kind to Animals Week

Fossils / 9–5
Listening Map / Be Kind to Animals Week

Hallelujah / 9–6, 9–7
Vocal/Instrumental Performance / Jewish Heritage Week

That's What Mothers Are Made of / 9–8
Composition Project / Mother's Day, Second Sunday in May

Brahms's Lullaby / 9–9
Music Reading Activity / Johannes Brahms, May 7

You Can't Top My Limerick / 9–10, 9–11
Composition Project / Limerick Day, May 12

The Stars and Stripes Forever / 9–12, 9–13
Listening Map / The Stars and Stripes Forever Day, May 14

Brave Americans / 9–14
    Two-Part Harmony / Memorial Day

Flowering Rhythms / 9–15
    Rhythm Dictation

JUNE
page 197

Dive on in, the Water's Fine! / 10–1
    Rhythm Dictation

Thank You, Teachers / 10–2
    Vocal Improvisation, Call and Response / Teacher Thank You Week

A Father's Day Song / 10–3
    Composition Project / Father's Day, Third Sunday in June

Hooray, Hooray! / 10–4
    Improvisation Activity / End of School

Hopping from Form to Form / 10–5
    Listening Guide: Musical Forms / End of School

Catch a Fish / 10–6
    Music Reading Activity

JULY
page 207

Have a Picnic! / 11–1
    Listening Guide: Musical Forms

Who Is Satchmo? / 11–2
    Research Project / Louis Armstrong, July 4

This Land Is Your Land / 11–3, 11–4
    Vocal/Instrumental Performance / Woody Guthrie, July 14

Yankee Doodle / 11–5
    Music Reading Activity / Independence Day, July 4

Teddy Bear, Teddy Bear / 11–6
    Musical Map / All-American Teddy Bear's Picnic

A Singing Telegram / 11–7
    Composition Exercise / Singing Telegram Birthday, July 28

What Baseball's About / 11–8, 11–9
Rhythmic Chant with Accompaniment

Catch a Fly / 11–10
Bass Clef Activity

AUGUST
page 223

I'm a Clown / 12–1, 12–2
Composition/Conducting Activity / National Clown Week

Sing and Conduct / 12–3
Conducting Activity

Music of the Sitar / 12–4, 12–5
Study Guide / India Independence Day, August 15

Discovering Impressionism / 12–6
Art Integration Activity / Claude Debussy, August 22

The Ants Go Marching / 12–7
Harmony Activity

Tennis, Anyone? / 12–8
Pitch Reading Activity

Canoeing Fun / 12–9
Rhythm Reading Activity

Back to School / 12–10
Rhythm Reading Activity

INDEXES
page 238

Alphabetical Index of Titles / page 238
Composers Index / page 239
Skills Index / page 239

SEPTEMBER

SEPTEMBER
TEACHER'S GUIDE

1–1, 1–2 **Grandmas Are Like That, Grandpas Are Like That**
Grandparent's Day, Second Sunday of September

GRADE LEVEL: 2–3

OBJECTIVE: Students will add lyrics and melodies to complete a song.

MATERIALS: Masters 1–1, 1–2

PREPARATION: Make student copies of Master 1–1 and/or Master 1–2.

DIRECTIONS: Use this exercise as a class or individual activity. Distribute student copies. Help students read and sing the printed portions of the song as follows:

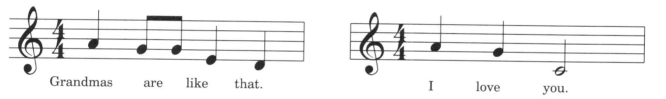

Encourage students to add words and melodies to fill in the spaces. Help students notate their melodies using iconic or traditional notation. For example:

Invite students to share their songs with the class. Encourage them to draw pictures as directed, and to give their songs to their grandparents as Grandparent's Day gifts.

1–3, 1–4 **Sing of Peace**
International Day of Peace, September 15

GRADE LEVEL: 4–6

MATERIALS: Masters 1–3, 1–4; resonator bells

OBJECTIVE: Students will perform a round with chordal accompaniment.

1–3, 1–4, Sing of Peace, continued

PREPARATION: Make student copies of the song, Master 1–3. Make a transparency and student copies of Master 1–4.

DIRECTIONS: Distribute student copies. Help students learn to sing the song. Sing in a two-, three-, or four- part round. Distribute resonator bells. Instruct students to find their pitches on the chord chart, to follow the chart, and to play whenever their pitches occur. Help students play bell tremolos, individually and then in sequence. Add the bell accompaniment to the round.

1–5 Admission: One Ticket Back to School

GRADE LEVEL: K–6

CLASSROOM MANAGEMENT IDEA: Seating chart

MATERIALS: Master 1–5

PREPARATION: Fill in your own name on the music class tickets. Duplicate one sheet for every class and cut tickets apart. Number your desks, chairs, or floor spaces to correspond with the ticket numbers.

DIRECTIONS: Distribute tickets before students enter the classroom. Instruct students to match their tickets to the chair numbers when they enter the room.

1–6 Give a Cheer!

GRADE LEVEL: 4–8

OBJECTIVE: Students will notate football cheers in traditional rhythmic notation.

MATERIALS: Master 1–6

PREPARATION: Make a transparency and student copies of Master 1–6.

DIRECTIONS: Open a discussion of about cheers heard at a football game. Invite students to share cheers that they know. Distribute copies of Master 1–6. Invite students to complete each example in traditional rhythmic notation. Provide correct answers for each example on the transparency. Assign as homework items 4–6 on the page. Invite students to share their cheers with the class. Encourage class members to help each other with correct notation.

1–7 Sounds of Autumn

GRADE LEVEL: 3–6

OBJECTIVE: Students will collect sound samples and create a sound piece.

MATERIALS: Master 1–7; several cassette recorders and tapes

PREPARATION: Make a transparency of Master 1–7.

DIRECTIONS: Invite students to think of sounds that they might hear in the fall of the year (for example, crackling leaves, school buses, a football game). Record student ideas on the transparency. Divide class into small groups, each equipped with a cassette recorder. Instruct groups to begin a sound scavenger hunt, recording as many sounds on the list as they can find. Combine tape-recorded examples onto a master tape. Help students edit, revise, and title their sound piece.

1–8 Counting Acorns

GRADE LEVEL: K–2

OBJECTIVE: Students will practice matching pitches.

MATERIALS: Master 1–8; four acorns, stones, erasers, or pieces of chalk; basket, coffee can, or container

PREPARATION: Teach the song by rote. Place three acorns (stones, chalk pieces, erasers) inside the basket.

DIRECTIONS: Invite students to form a circle. Choose one student to be the squirrel. The squirrel chooses the number of acorns to keep in the can and pretends to give any extras to the teacher. He or she then moves around the inside of the circle and points to each child as the class sings. At the * the squirrel stops in front of one child. That child sings the questions, guessing the number of acorns in the can. The squirrel responds with the appropriate answer. The questioner becomes the new squirrel, and the game begins again.

1–9 Rhapsody in Blue
George Gershwin, September 26, 1898

GRADE LEVEL: 4–8

OBJECTIVE: Students will identify the major themes in a musical example.

MATERIALS: Master 1–9; recording of George Gershwin's "Rhapsody in Blue"; four sheets of construction paper; markers

1–9, Rhapsody in Blue, continued

PREPARATION: Make a transparency of Master 1–9. Make large construction-paper letters: A, B, C, and D.

DIRECTIONS: Isolate the four major themes on your recording. Help students study the themes carefully, describing each in terms of melody, rhythm, timbre, and so forth. Divide the class into four groups, and give each group a letter: A, B, C, or D. Instruct students to listen to the entire composition and to stand when they hear their theme. Follow the themes on the transparency as students listen. On repeated listenings, use student copies of Master 1–9, and invite students to trace each theme as it is heard.

1–10 Canoe Song
Native American Day, Fourth Friday in September

GRADE LEVEL: 3–6

OBJECTIVE: Students will perform a round with instrumental accompaniment.

MATERIALS: Master 1–10; mallet instruments

PREPARATION: Make a transparency of Master 1–10.

DIRECTIONS: Display transparency. Teach or review the song. Divide the class into two groups and sing in a two-part round. Add instrumental parts to accompany the round.

1–11 Canoe Song
Native American Day, Fourth Friday in September

GRADE LEVEL: 2–3

OBJECTIVE: Students will read icons and play a melody.

MATERIALS: Master 1–11; bellsets; mallets

PREPARATION: Make a transparency and student copies of Master 1–11.

DIRECTIONS: Determine whether students will work individually or in small groups. Distribute student copies. Help students understand the directions. Allow time for students to read the icons and to play the song.

1–12 Names and Faces
Back to School

GRADE LEVEL: 3–6

OBJECTIVE: Students will create a rhythmic chant.

MATERIALS: Master 1–12; recording of instrumental selection in moderate 4/4 meter

PREPARATION: Make a transparency of Master 1–12.

DIRECTIONS: See Master 1–12.

1–13 Raking Leaves
Autumn

GRADE LEVEL: 1–4

OBJECTIVE: Students will perform a chant with movement.

MATERIALS: Master 1–13

PREPARATION: Make one copy of Master 1–13.

DIRECTIONS: Teach the chant by rote. At the end of verse one, begin to move the right hand to the beat. Continue moving the right hand and cumulatively add other body parts, moving to the beat. The challenge is to keep the body parts moving, to add new ones, and to continue chanting, all at the same time! Have fun!

Written by _____ **Especially for** _____ **Date** _____

1–1 **Grandmas Are Like That**

Grand-
mas are
like
that.

Grand-
mas are
like
that.

Grand-
mas are
like
that.

Grand-
mas are
like
that,
I
love
you!

A picture of Grandma and me

Written by _____ Especially for _____ Date _____

1–2   **Grandpas Are Like That**

Grand-
       pas are
               like
                    that.

Grand-
       pas are
               like
                    that.

Grand-
       pas are
               like
                    that.

Grand-
       pas are
               like
                    that,   I
                                     love
                                          you!

A picture of Grandpa and me

Name _____   Date _____

1–3   **Sing of Peace**

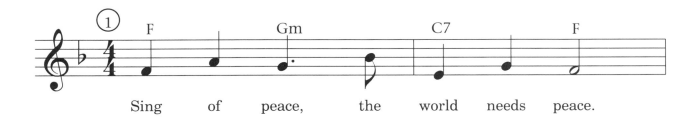

Sing   of   peace,   the   world   needs   peace.

Sing   of   peace,   the   world   needs   peace.

Neigh - bors   all,   great   and   small,   live   in   har - mo - ny.

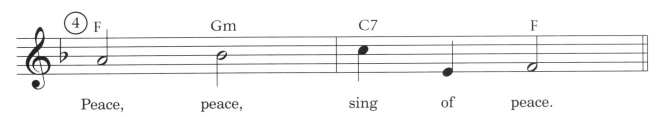

Peace,   peace,   sing   of   peace.

1–4   **Sing of Peace**

```
    C                   D                   B♭                  C
    A                   B♭                  G                   A
    F                   G                   E                   F
                                            C
  Sing      of      peace,      the      world     needs     peace.


    C                   D                   B♭                  C
    A                   B♭                  G                   A
    F                   G                   E                   F
                                            C
  Sing      of      peace,      the      world     needs     peace.


    C                   D                   B♭                  C
    A                   B♭                  G                   A
    F                   G                   E                   F
                                            C
 Neigh-bors  all,   great    and    small,    live    in   har-  mo-  ny.


    C                   D                   B♭                  C
    A                   B♭                  G                   A
    F                   G                   E                   F
                                            C
  Peace,              peace,           sing     of           peace.
```

1–5   # Admission: One Ticket

ADMIT ONE _____'S MUSIC CLASS RESERVED SEAT #1	ADMIT ONE _____'S MUSIC CLASS RESERVED SEAT #2	ADMIT ONE _____'S MUSIC CLASS RESERVED SEAT #3	ADMIT ONE _____'S MUSIC CLASS RESERVED SEAT #4
ADMIT ONE _____'S MUSIC CLASS RESERVED SEAT #5	ADMIT ONE _____'S MUSIC CLASS RESERVED SEAT #6	ADMIT ONE _____'S MUSIC CLASS RESERVED SEAT #7	ADMIT ONE _____'S MUSIC CLASS RESERVED SEAT #8
ADMIT ONE _____'S MUSIC CLASS RESERVED SEAT #9	ADMIT ONE _____'S MUSIC CLASS RESERVED SEAT #10	ADMIT ONE _____'S MUSIC CLASS RESERVED SEAT #11	ADMIT ONE _____'S MUSIC CLASS RESERVED SEAT #12
ADMIT ONE _____'S MUSIC CLASS RESERVED SEAT #13	ADMIT ONE _____'S MUSIC CLASS RESERVED SEAT #14	ADMIT ONE _____'S MUSIC CLASS RESERVED SEAT #15	ADMIT ONE _____'S MUSIC CLASS RESERVED SEAT #16
ADMIT ONE _____'S MUSIC CLASS RESERVED SEAT #17	ADMIT ONE _____'S MUSIC CLASS RESERVED SEAT #18	ADMIT ONE _____'S MUSIC CLASS RESERVED SEAT #19	ADMIT ONE _____'S MUSIC CLASS RESERVED SEAT #20
ADMIT ONE _____'S MUSIC CLASS RESERVED SEAT #21	ADMIT ONE _____'S MUSIC CLASS RESERVED SEAT #22	ADMIT ONE _____'S MUSIC CLASS RESERVED SEAT #23	ADMIT ONE _____'S MUSIC CLASS RESERVED SEAT #24
ADMIT ONE _____'S MUSIC CLASS RESERVED SEAT #25	ADMIT ONE _____'S MUSIC CLASS RESERVED SEAT #26	ADMIT ONE _____'S MUSIC CLASS RESERVED SEAT #27	ADMIT ONE _____'S MUSIC CLASS RESERVED SEAT #28
ADMIT ONE _____'S MUSIC CLASS RESERVED SEAT #29	ADMIT ONE _____'S MUSIC CLASS RESERVED SEAT #30	ADMIT ONE _____'S MUSIC CLASS RESERVED SEAT #31	ADMIT ONE _____'S MUSIC CLASS RESERVED SEAT #32
ADMIT ONE _____'S MUSIC CLASS RESERVED SEAT #33	ADMIT ONE _____'S MUSIC CLASS RESERVED SEAT #34	ADMIT ONE _____'S MUSIC CLASS RESERVED SEAT #35	ADMIT ONE _____'S MUSIC CLASS RESERVED SEAT #36

Name _____ **Date** _____

1–6   Give A Cheer!

Learn these football cheers. Study their musical notation.

1.   F - I - G - H - T!   F - I - G - H - T,   fight, fight, fight.

2. Block   that   kick!   Block   that   kick!

3. Touch - down,   touch - down,   we   want   a   touch - down.

Find three more football cheers. Write them below. Write each cheer in musical notation.

4.

5.

6.

Name _____   Date _____

1–7   **Sounds Of Autumn**

Directions: Think of sounds that you might hear in the fall of the year. Write your sounds on these leaves. Take a cassette recorder outdoors for a scavenger hunt. Find as many of your sounds as you can. Record the sounds on a tape. Edit your tape to create a musical sound piece.

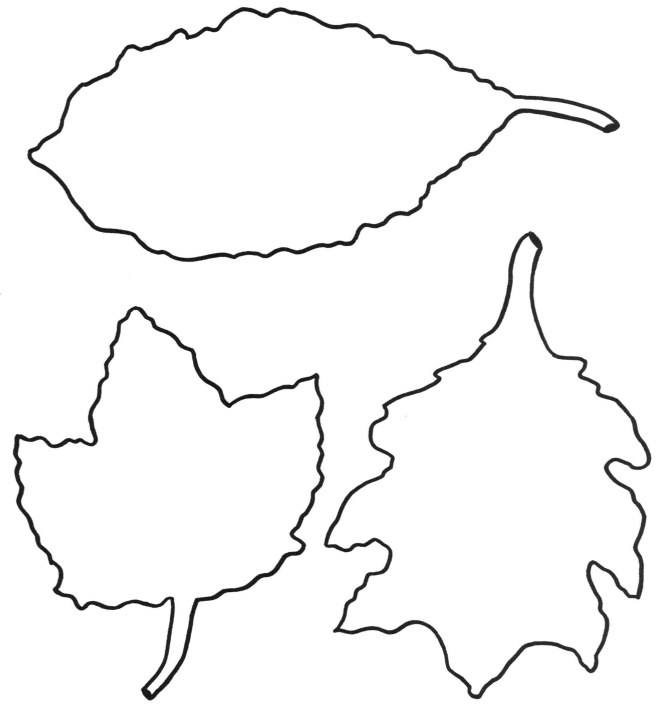

Name _____   **Date** _____

1–8  **Counting Acorns**

Squir - rel,   squir - rel,   come   with   me

come   in - side   my   a - corn   tree.

Guess   a   num - ber,   one,   two,   three,

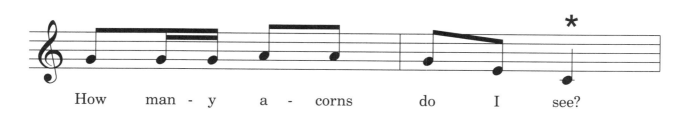

How   man - y   a - corns   do   I   see?

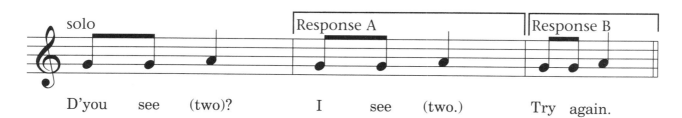

D'you   see   (two)?   I   see   (two.)   Try   again.

Name _____   Date _____

1–9

Rhapsody in Blue*
by George Gershwin

Theme A

Theme B

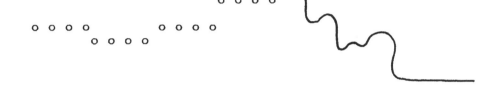

Theme C

Theme D

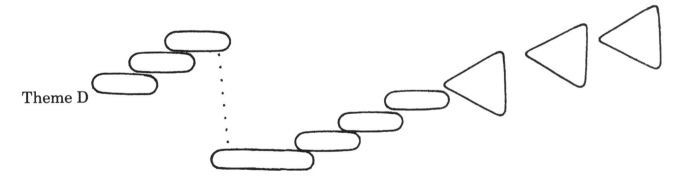

Name _____ **Date** _____

1–10

Canoe Song

My pad - dle's keen and bright, Flash-ing with sil - ver.

Fol - low the wild goose flight, Dip, dip, and swing.

Accompany this song with these patterns:

Alto Glockenspiel

Alto Xylophone

Bass Xylophone

Instrumental accompaniments by Jane Frazee, Director, University of St. Thomas Institute for Contemporary Music Education.

1–11　　　　　　　　**Canoe Song**

mi

My　　pad-

re

dle's

do

keen

la,

and

bright,

la

ver.

mi

sil-

re

with

do

Flash-

ing

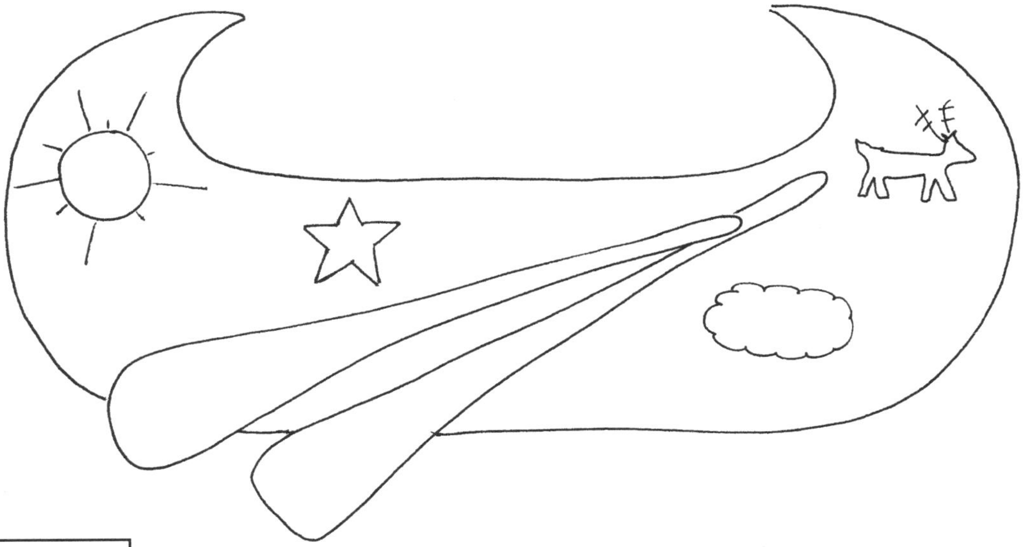

mi

Fol-

low

re

the

do

wild

la,

goose

flight,

la,

Dip,　　dip,

sol,

and

swing.

© 1992 by Loretta Mitchell

1–12   **Names and Faces**

1. Sit in a circle. Keep the beat by clapping, snapping fingers, or tapping.
2. Choose one person's first name and last name to begin.
3. Use this rhythm pattern to create a name chant.

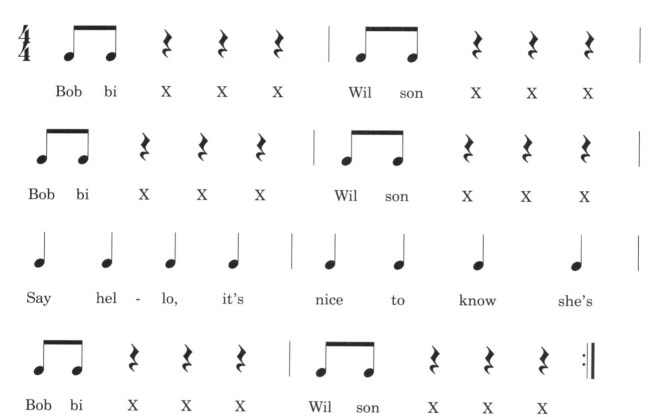

Bob bi X X X Wil son X X X

Bob bi X X X Wil son X X X

Say hel - lo, it's nice to know she's

Bob bi X X X Wil son X X X

4. Without losing a beat, move to the next person to the left. Continue with a rhythm pattern using the next person's name.

5. Add recorded music to your chant.

Name _____ **Date** _____

1–13   **Raking Leaves**

Rak - ing   leaves   a   bush - el   at   a   time.

Pay   that   ra - ker   a   nick - el   or   a   dime.

Take   all   day   or   add   an - oth - er   rake,

Hold   it   with   your   *right hand,* be - fore   you   take   a   break.

2. Left hand
3. Right foot
4. Left foot
5. Chin

Other variations: elbows, knee caps, shoulder

OCTOBER
TEACHER'S GUIDE

2-1 Bushels of Apples
National Apple Month

GRADE LEVEL: 2–4

OBJECTIVE: Students will compose a pentatonic song.

MATERIALS: Master 2–1; bellsets

PREPARATION: Make a transparency and student copies of Master 2–1.

DIRECTIONS: Help students read the rhyme. Chant the words and clap the beat. Chant the words and tap the rhythm. Read and clarify the instructions for the class. Model a sample composition, writing the pitches on your transparency. Allow time for students to complete their compositions. Encourage students to perform for the class.

2-2 Popping, Popping
National Popcorn Poppin' Month

GRADE LEVEL: 2–4

OBJECTIVE: Students will compose a pentatonic song.

MATERIALS: Master 2–2; bellsets

PREPARATION: Make a transparency and student copies of Master 2–2.

DIRECTIONS: Chant the words of the rhyme with the class. Help students clap the beat as they chant. Help students tap the rhythm of the words as they chant the words again. Model a sample melody. Write your melody on the transparency, using solfège syllables, letter names, or scale numbers. Allow time for students to compose their own melodies. To extend the activity, encourage students to create an instrumental accompaniment for the song.

2-3 Christopher Columbus
Columbus Day, October 12

GRADE LEVEL: 2–4

OBJECTIVE: The student will compose a melody using sol, mi, and la.

MATERIALS: Master 2–3; bellsets

PREPARATION: Make a transparency and student copies of Master 2–3.

DIRECTIONS: Chant the words with the class. Help students clap the beat as they chant. Help students tap the rhythm of the words as they chant the words again. Model a sample melody. Write the sample melody on your transparency using syllables, letter names, or scale numbers. Allow time for students to compose their own melodies. Encourage students to modify the song rhythm to fit the lyrics of the second verse and to create a third verse for the song.

2–4, 2–5 Who Stowed Away?
Columbus Day, October 12

GRADE LEVEL: 1–3

OBJECTIVE: Students will practice matching pitches and identify classmates' singing voices.

MATERIALS: Masters 2–4, 2–5

PREPARATION: Make three copies of Master 2–5. Write *Niña* on one ship, *Pinta* on the second, and *Santa Maria* on the third. Place the ships on the floor in the back of the classroom.

DIRECTIONS: Help the class learn the song (Master 2–4). Sing the solo responses yourself. Ask for volunteers to sing the solos. When the class knows the song well, play the game as follows: (a) Select three soloists. Send them to the back of the room, select a ship, and stand on it. (b) Instruct the class members to remain facing the front. (c) Sing the song with the soloists. (d) Ask volunteers to guess which child sang each solo. (e) Allow correct guessers to become soloists as you repeat the game.

2–6 Three Billy Goats Gruff
Opening of the Metropolitan Opera House, October 22,1883

GRADE LEVEL: 2–4

OBJECTIVE: Students will improvise melodies and create an opera.

MATERIALS: Master 2–6

PREPARATION: Make student copies of the script, Master 2–6.

DIRECTIONS: Select students for each character in the play. Read through the play using speaking voices. Discuss the features of an opera. Model improvised musical conversation. Select one or two lines of the script and model improvised melodies. Help students improvise melodies for each of their lines. Rehearse the opera. Repeat with other students playing the characters.

2–7, 2–8   Songs from Around the World
United Nations Day, October 24

GRADE LEVEL: 4–6

OBJECTIVE: Students will find songs of the world and locate their countries of origin on a world map.

MATERIALS: Masters 2–7, 2–8; music texts; resource books

PREPARATION: Make transparencies and student copies of Masters 2–7 and 2–8. Locate resource books for students to use.

DIRECTIONS: Clarify instructions with the class. Divide the class into groups of three or four. Set up guidelines to help groups to work cooperatively. Help the class pool their song lists. List all songs on Transparency 2–7, and mark all countries of origin on Transparency 2–8. Sing as many of the songs as time permits.

2–9   Ten Little Costumes
Halloween, October 31

GRADE LEVEL: K–2

OBJECTIVE: Students will play a rhythm game.

MATERIALS: Master 2–9

PREPARATION: Make one copy of Master 2–9.

DIRECTIONS: Help students learn the rhyme by rote. Invite students to form a circle. Choose one student to be "IT." IT skips around the inside of the circle and points to each child as the class chants. On the word "YOU," IT chooses a new IT, and the game begins again, with "Nine little costumes . . . ."

2–10, 2–11   Little Orphant Annie
Halloween, October 31

GRADE LEVEL: 4–6

OBJECTIVE: Students will perform a choral reading with instrumental accompaniment. Students will create a melody.

MATERIALS: Masters 2–10, 2–11; rhythm instruments

PREPARATION: Make student copies of Masters 2–10 and 2–11.

DIRECTIONS: Invite students to read through the poem. Practice the last line of each stanza "An' the gobble-uns . . ." to learn the rhythm and add effective expression. Help students listen to four different rhythm instruments and select one or more to accompany the last line of each stanza. Assign parts. Rehearse. Discuss changes to make the performance more effective. Perform the reading again.

EXTENSION: Help students create a melody line for the last line of each stanza " An' the gobble-uns . . ." Sing the last line as you perform the poem.

2–12, 2–13 Nine Lives
Halloween, October 31

GRADE LEVEL: 2–3

OBJECTIVE: Students will read, sing, and play a melody.

MATERIALS: Masters 2–12, 2–13; bellsets; mallets

PREPARATION: Make student copies of Masters 2–12 and 2–13.

DIRECTIONS: Distribute student copies of Master 2–12. Invite students to read the song and sing it. When students know the song well, distribute bellsets and copies of Master 2–13. Invite students to follow the page directions and learn to play the song.

2–14, 2–15 Black and Gold
Halloween, October 31

GRADE LEVEL: 3–5

OBJECTIVE: Students will play chords to accompany a song.

MATERIALS: Masters 2–14, 2–15; resonator bells, markers

PREPARATION: Make transparencies of Masters 2–14 and 2–15. Color pitch circles as follows: D = orange, F = yellow, A = blue, G = green, B♭ = red, C♯ = brown, E = purple.

2–14, 2–15, Black and Gold, continued

DIRECTIONS:	Teach or review the song "Black and Gold." When students can sing it well, distribute resonator bells. Show students how to create a tremolo sound on their bells. Help students understand the chord chart transparency. Practice playing one chord at a time and putting the chords into sequence. Add the bell accompaniment to the song.

2–16 Trick or Treat
Halloween, October 31

GRADE LEVEL:	3–5
OBJECTIVE:	Students will sing partner songs.
MATERIALS:	Masters 2–14, 2–16; bellsets
PREPARATION:	Make a transparency or student copies of Master 2–16. Review "Black and Gold," Master 2–14.
DIRECTIONS:	Help students learn the song "Trick or Treat." When they can sing it without assistance, help them sing it as a partner song to "Black and Gold."
EXTENSION:	Add the bell accompaniment, Master 2–15.

2–17, 2–18, Caught in a Spider Web
2-19 Halloween, October 31

GRADE LEVEL:	3–6
OBJECTIVE:	Students will review treble clef letter names.
MATERIALS:	Masters 2–17, 2–18, 2–19; game pieces; dice
PREPARATION:	Make student copies of Master 2–17 (one per group). Duplicate Spider Web cards, Master 2–18 (one set per group) and Treble Clef cards, Master 2–19 (one set per group). Use two different colors of paper for the card sets. Cut cards apart. Secure three to four kinds of game pieces for the players (for example, pennies, nickels, dimes, and quarters or sets of four different buttons). Make or find dice (traditional or musical), one die for each group.
DIRECTIONS:	Divide class into small groups (three to four members). Read the following rules aloud.
	Sit in a circle with game board in the center. Place Spider Web cards and Treble Clef cards in their places on the board. Play will move clockwise around the circle. Choose your game piece. The player who chooses

_____ *will be first. Player #1 rolls the die and moves the indicated number of squares. A player who lands on a treble clef sign must draw a Treble Clef card and name the note correctly or go back to start. A player who lands on a spider web sign must draw a Spider Web card and follow the instructions or go back to Start. The first player to reach "Fine" is the winner.*

2–20, 2–21	**Halloween Rondo** **Halloween, October 31**
GRADE LEVEL:	3–5
OBJECTIVE:	Students will perform a rondo.
MATERIALS:	Masters 2–20, 2–21; classroom instruments
PREPARATION:	Make a transparency (and optional student copies) of Master 2–20. Make a transparency and student copies of Master 2–21.
DIRECTIONS:	Help students read the rhyme expressively and rhythmically. Select soloists or small groups to read Part B and Part C. Put the parts together in a rondo form:

A   B   A   C   A

Discuss possibilities for instrumental accompaniment. Add instruments as suggested by students. Discuss possibilities for variations in expressive elements (tempo, dynamics, vocal expression). Add changes to make the rondo most effective. Distribute copies of Master 2–21. Help students create a visual rondo by adding creepy, crawly things to the rondo map.

Name _____   **Date** _____

Bushels of Apples

Compose a song about apples. Use these bells.

| C | D | E | G | A |

Write your pitches above the words.
Practice singing and playing your song.

Bush- els   and   bush- els   and   bush- els   of   ap -   ples.

Bush- els   and   bush- els   and   bush- els   I   see.

Bush- els   and   bush- els   and   bush- els   of   ap -   ples.

Hope   that   my   mom   bakes   a   pie   for   me.

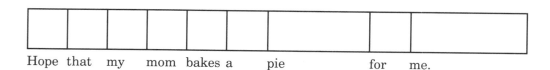

Name _____   **Date** _____

2–2   **Popping, Popping**

Compose a popcorn song. Use these bells.

| C | D | E | G | A |

Write your pitches above the words.
Practice singing and playing your song.

Pop-	ping,	pop-	ping,	hear	it	pop!

I	can't	wait	'til	it	will	stop!

I'll	have	two	bags,	three,	or	four.

When	they're	gone,	I'll	have	some	more.

Name _____   **Date** _____

2–3   **Christopher Columbus**

1. Compose a song about Christopher Columbus. Use these bells.

E   G   A

Write your pitches above the words. Practice singing and playing your song.

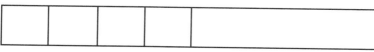

Chris- to - pher Co - lum - bus

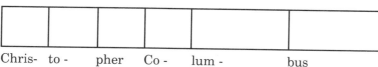

Had a might- y dream.

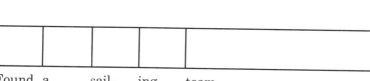

Chris- to - pher Co - lum - bus

Found a sail- ing team.

2. Change the rhythm of the song to fit the words of verse two:

      Isabella, Isabella,
      Queen of elegance,
      Isabella, Isabella,
      Thought she'd take a chance.

3. Make up a third verse for the song.

Name _____   Date _____

2–4   **Who Stowed Away?**

Get your coat and hat. There's no time to chat.

Take a trip on a sailing ship, The world cannot be flat.

solo 1
Who's on the Ni - ña? I'm on the Ni - ña.

class   solo 2
Who's on the Pin - ta? I'm on the Pin - ta.

class
Who stowed a - way on the San - ta Mar - i - a?

solo 3
I stowed a - way on the San - ta Mar - i - a.

2–5   **Who Stowed Away?**

Directions: Make three copies of this page. Label the ships the *Niña*, the *Pinta*, and the *Santa Maria*. Color, cut out the ships, and laminate if desired.

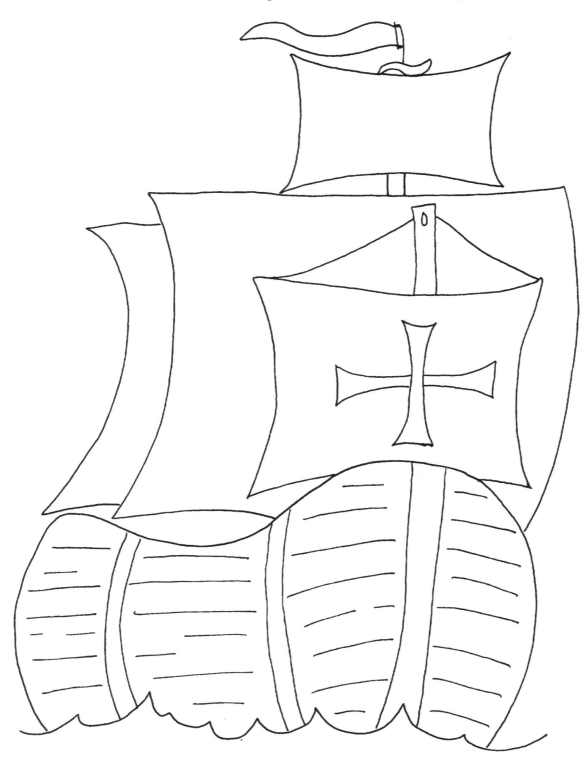

Name _____   Date _____

2–6   **Three Billy Goats Gruff**

Narrator 1:	Once upon a time there were three billy goats.
First Billy Goat:	I am the first billy goat. I am very small.
Second Billy Goat:	I am the second billy goat. I am a little larger.
Third Billy Goat:	I am the third billy goat. I am very large.
Narrator 2:	Every day they went to the meadow to eat green grass. Green grass was good for them and helped them grow bigger and stronger.
Narrator 3:	But to get to the meadow, they had to cross a bridge.
Narrator 1:	Under the bridge lived a grouchy troll.
Troll:	I am the grouchy troll. No one crosses my bridge.
Narrator 2:	In spite of the troll's warning, the goats tiptoed across the bridge, one by one.
Narrator 3:	The first goat crossed the bridge.
First Billy Goat:	Tip, toe, tip, toe, I can cross this bridge.

2–6, Three Billy Goats Gruff, continued

Troll:	Who's that tiptoeing across my bridge?
First Billy Goat:	It is I, the first billy goat. I'm going to the meadow to eat green grass because it is good for me.
Troll:	I am going to eat you.
First Billy Goat:	Oh please, wait for the second billy goat who is much larger than I am.
Troll:	Very well, be off with you.
Narrator 1:	The second goat crossed the bridge.
Second Billy Goat:	Tip, toe, tip, toe, I can cross this bridge.
Troll:	Who's that tiptoeing across my bridge?
Second Billy Goat:	It is I, the second billy goat. I'm going to the meadow to eat green grass because it is good for me.
Troll:	I am going to eat you.
Second Billy Goat:	Oh please, wait for the third billy goat who is much larger than I am.
Troll:	Very well, be off with you.
Narrator 2:	The third goat crossed the bridge.
Third Billy Goat:	Tip, toe, tip, toe, I can cross this bridge.
Troll:	Who's that tiptoeing across my bridge?
Third Billy Goat:	It is I, the third billy goat. I'm going to the meadow to eat green grass because it is good for me.
Troll:	I am going to eat you.
Third Billy Goat:	Come on up and try it. I am bigger than you. You can't eat me.
Narrator 3:	The troll came up on the bridge. The third goat butted him up into the air, and he was never seen again.
Narrator 1:	The third goat continued on his way to the meadow to eat green grass because it was good for him.
Narrator 2:	From that day, the three billy goats crossed the bridge whenever they wished.
Narrator 3:	They ate green grass to their hearts' content and lived healthily ever after.

THE END

Name _____   Date _____

2–7   **Songs from Around the World**

Directions: (1) Select a member of the group for each job: recorder, reader, and map marker. (2) Use the resource books provided by your teacher. Find as many songs as you can from around the world. Record each song in the spaces below. Put a star on the world map to locate the country of origin for each song. Sing the songs.

SONG TITLE	COUNTRY OF ORIGIN	RESOURCE BOOK AND PAGE

© 1992 by Loretta Mitchell

Name _____

Date _____

Songs from Around the World

2–8

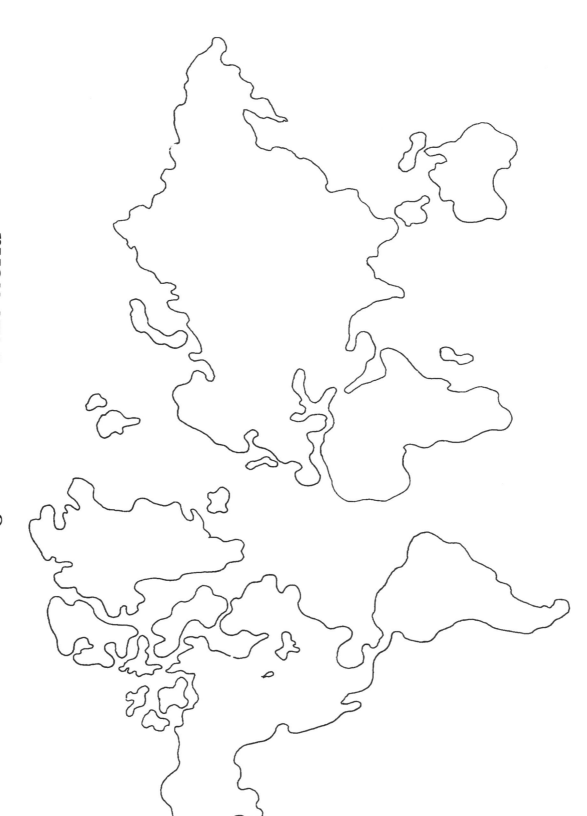

Name _____   **Date** _____

2–9   **Ten Little Costumes**

$\frac{2}{4}$

Ten lit-tle cos-tumes at the cos-tume store,

Ten lit-tle cos-tumes, who could ask for more?

I want first pick, you do, too.

Dou-ble trou-ble in a bub-ble, I pick YOU!

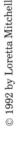

Name _____   **Date** _____

2–10   **Little Orphant Annie***

CHILDREN 1–6: Little Orphant Annie's come to our house to stay,

CHILD 1: To wash the cups an' saucers up,

CHILD 2: An' brush the crumbs away,

CHILD 3: An' shoo the chickens off the porch,

CHILD 4: An' dust the hearth,

CHILD 5: An' sweep,

CHILD 6: An' make the fire,

CHILD 1: An' bake the bread,

CHILD 2: An' earn her board-an-keep;

CHILDREN 1–6: An' all us other children, when the supper things is done,
We sit around the kitchen fire an' has the mostest fun,

CHILD 3: A-list-nin' to the witch-tales 'at Annie tells about,

CLASS: AN' THE   GOBBLE-UNS 'LL GITS YOU

EF YOU   DON'T   WATCH   OUT!

© 1992 by Loretta Mitchell

* Adapted from "Little Orphant Annie" from THE COMPLETE WORKS OF JAMES WHITCOMB RILEY, Vol. 3, edited by Edmund Henry
Eitel (Indianapolis, Bobbs-Merrill, 1913).

2–10, Little Orphant Annie, continued

CHILDREN 1–6:   Onc't they was a little boy wouldn't say his prayers,

CHILD 1:   An' when he went to bed at night, away upstairs,

CHILD 2:   His mammy heerd him holler,

CHILD 3:   An' his daddy heerd him bawl,

CHILD 4:   An' when they turn't the kivvers down,

CHILDREN 4–6:   He wasn't there at all!

CHILD 5:   An' they seeked him in the rafter room,

CHILD 6:   An' cubby-hole,

CHILD 1:   An' press,

CHILD 2:   An' seeked him up the chimbley-flue,

CHILD 3:   An' ever'where, I guess;

CHILDREN 1–6:   But all they ever found was thist his pants an' roundabout:

CLASS: AN' THE   GOBBLE-UNS 'LL GIT YOU

EF   YOU   DON'T   WATCH   OUT!

Name _____ **Date** _____

2–11 **Little Orphant Annie***

CHILDREN 1–6: An'one time a little girl 'ud allus laugh an' grin,

CHILD 1: An' make fun of ever'one,

CHILD 2: An' all her blood an' kin;

CHILD 3: An' onc't when they was "company,"

CHILD 4: An' old folks was there,

CHILD 5: She mocked 'em

CHILD 6: An' shocked 'em,

CHILDREN 4–6: An' said she didn't care!

CHILD 1: An' thist as she kicked her heels,

CHILD 2: An' turn't to run an' hide,

CHILD 3: They was two great big Black Things a-standin' by her side,

CHILDREN 1–6: An' they snatched her through the ceilin' 'fore she knowed what she's about!

CLASS:

*Adapted for choral reading from the original poem by James Whitcomb Riley.

2–11, Little Orphant Annie, continued

CHILDREN 1–6: An' little Orphant Annie says, when the blaze is blue,

CHILD 1: An' the lamp wick sputters,

CHILD 2: An' the wind goes woo-oo!

CHILD 3: An' you hear the crickets quit,

CHILD 4: An' the moon is gray,

CHILD 5: An' the lightnin' bugs in dew is all squenched away,

CHILD 6: You better mind yer parents,

CHILD 1: An' yer teachers fond an' dear,

CHILD 2: An' churish them 'at loves you,

CHILD 3: An' dry the orphant's tear,

CHILDREN 4–6: An' he'p the pore an' needy one, 'at clusters all about,

CLASS: ER' THE GOBBLE-UNS 'LL GIT YOU EF YOU DON'T WATCH OUT!

Name _____   **Date** _____

2–12   **Nine Lives**

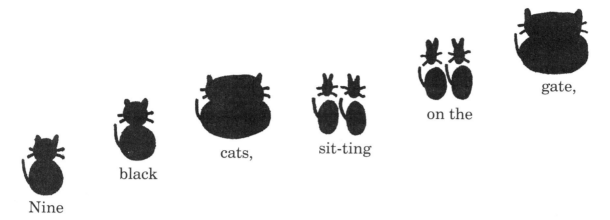

Nine   black   cats,   sit-ting   on the   gate,

One   caught a   cold   and   then   there were   eight.

2. Eight black cats looking up to heaven,
   One lost its balance, and then there were seven.
3. Seven black cats gathering sticks,
   One got a splinter, and then there were six.
4. Six black cats trying to survive,
   One lost its courage, and then there were five.
5. Five black cats knocking at the door,
   One rang the bell, and then there were four.
6. Four black cats climbing up a tree,
   One lost its grip, and then there were three.
7. Three black cats feeling kinda blue,
   One stubbed its paw, and then there were two.
8. Two black cats, sitting in the sun,
   One got a sunburn, and then there was one.
9. One black cat, twitched its magic nose,
   Wished for nine more lives, and what do you suppose?
Go back to verse one, and start again!

2-13   **Nine Lives**

Directions: Learn to sing and play this song.

D	E	F	F	F	G	G	A
la Nine	ti black	do cats,	do sit -	do ting	re on	re the	mi gate,

A	A	A	A	G	F	E	E	D
mi One	mi caught	mi a	mi cold	re and	do then	ti there	ti were	la eight.

2. Eight black cats looking up to heaven,
   One lost its balance, and then there were seven.

3. Seven black cats gathering sticks,
   One got a splinter, and then there were six.

4. Six black cats trying to survive,
   One lost its courage, and then there were five.

5. Five black cats knocking at the door,
   One rang the bell, and then there were four.

6. Four black cats climbing up a tree,
   One lost its grip, and then there were three.

7. Three black cats feeling kinda blue,
   One stubbed its paw, and then there were two.

8. Two black cats, sitting in the sun,
   One got a sunburn, and then there was one.

9. One black cat, twitched its magic nose,
   Wished for nine more lives, and what do you suppose?

Go back to verse one, and start again!

Name _____   Date _____

2–14   **Black and Gold***

Music by Michael Stevens
Words by Nancy Byrd Turner

Ev'-ry-thing is black and gold,

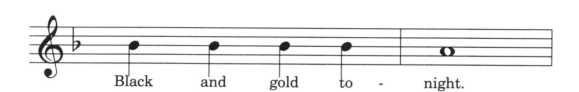

Black and gold to - night.

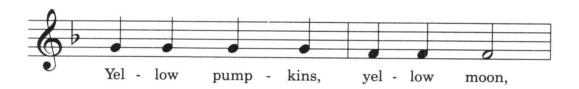

Yel - low pump - kins, yel - low moon,

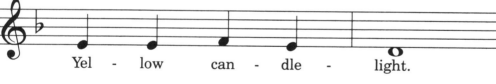

Yel - low can - dle - light.

2–15

Black and Gold Harmony*

Music by Michael Stevens
Words by Nancy Byrd Turner

A F D **Dm**	A F D **Dm**	A F D **Dm**	A F D **Dm**
Ev'ry-	thing is	black and	gold,
D B♭ G **Gm**	D B♭ G **Gm**	A F D **Dm**	A F D **Dm**
Black and	gold to-	night.	
D B♭ G **Gm**	D B♭ G **Gm**	A F D **Dm**	A F D **Dm**
Yel-low	pump-kins,	yel-low	moon,
D B♭ G **Gm**	G E C# A **A7**	A F D **Dm**	A F D **Dm**
Yel-low	can-dle	light.	

Name _____ **Date** _____

2–16 **Trick or Treat**

Knock on doors and have some fun.

Hur - ry down the street.

Each Oct - o - ber Thir - ty One,

Time for Trick or Treat.

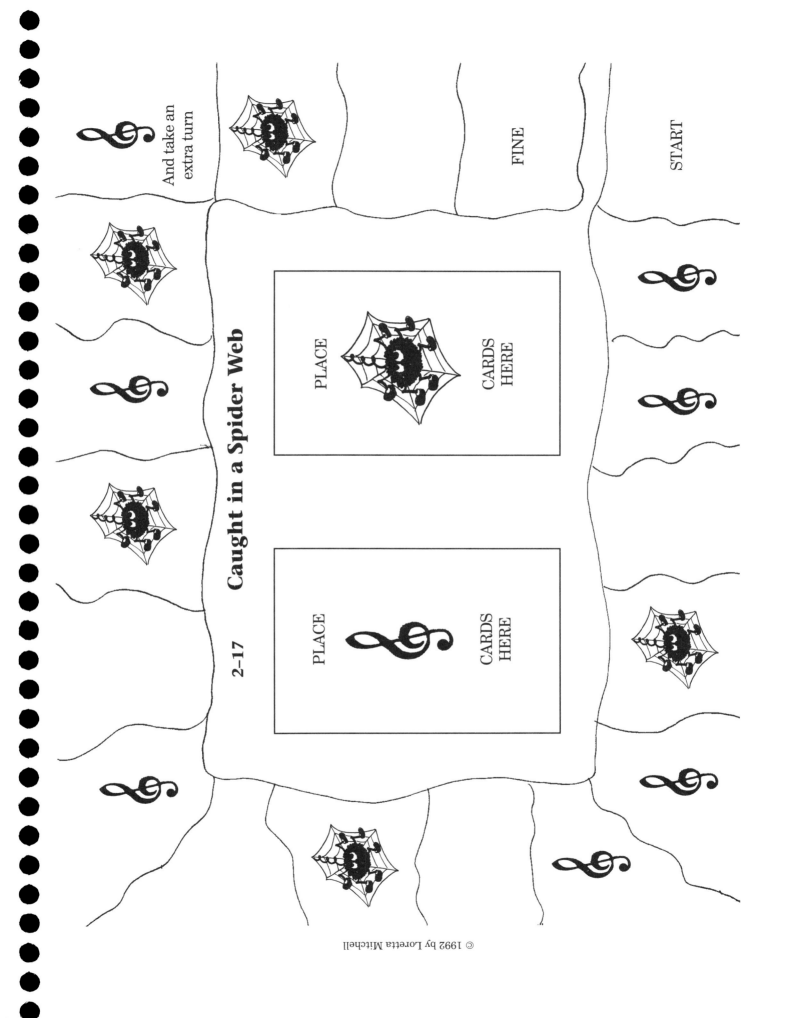

Caught in a Spider Web

2-17

PLACE — CARDS HERE

PLACE — CARDS HERE

And take an extra turn

FINE

START

Caught in a Spider Web

2-18

Clap a rhythm pattern for the other players to echo. Advance three spaces.

Go back to START.

Lose one turn.

Advance two spaces.

Advance three spaces.

Hum the first line of a song. If another player can guess its title advance four spaces.

Advance one space.

Name a famous composer or go back two spaces.

Go back one space.

Caught in a Spider Web

Name _____

Date _____

2-19

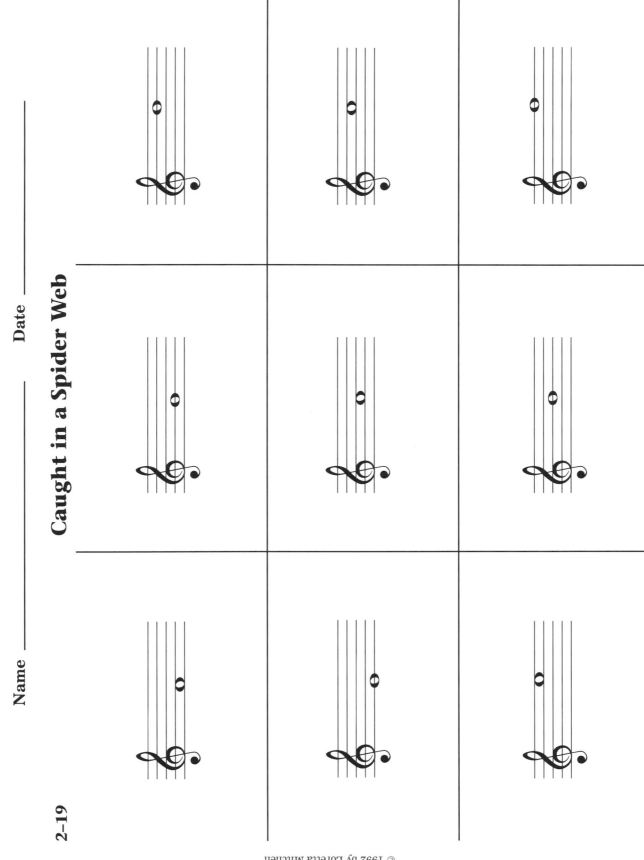

Name _____   Date _____

2–20   **Halloween Rondo**

PART A
    Creepy, crawly, squirmy things
    Things of slimy green.
    Add them to my pot of stew,
    Tonight is Halloween.

PART B
    Spiders and a spider web,
    Sparrow's nest and moss.
    Dragonflies and centipedes,
    In the kettle toss.

PART C
    Lizards topped with mustard sauce,
    Bubble gum that's chewed.
    Tarantulas and ladybugs,
    What delicious food!

Name _____   Date _____

2–21

Halloween Rondo

Directions: Make a picture of your rondo. Add your own creatures to complete this map.

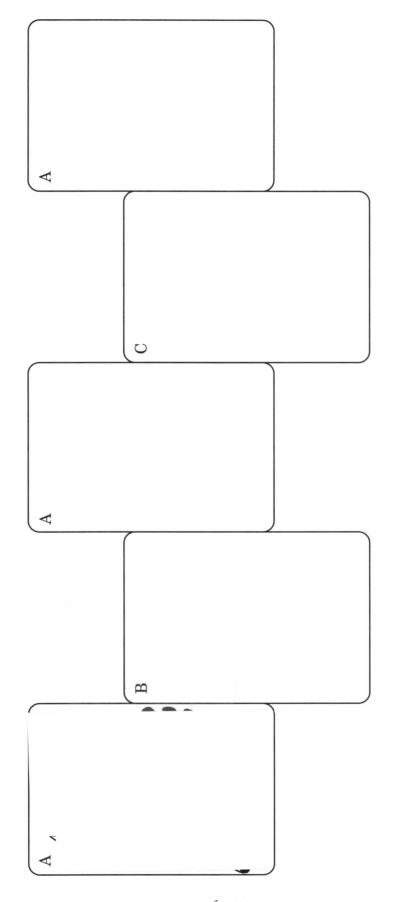

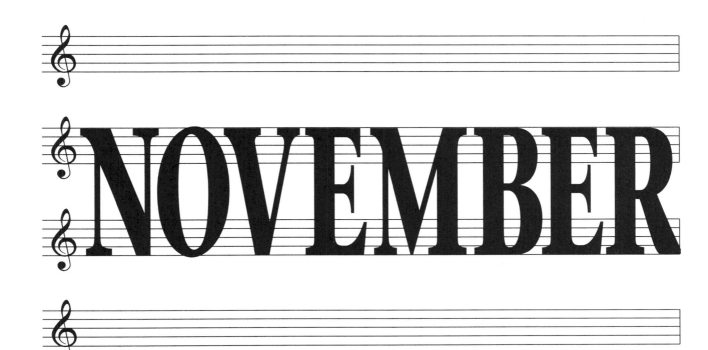

NOVEMBER
TEACHER'S GUIDE

3–1 Extra! Extra! Our School Is Great!
American Education Week

GRADE LEVEL: 4–6

OBJECTIVE: Students will perform a speech composition.

MATERIALS: Master 3–1; newspapers (optional)

PREPARATION: Make student copies of Master 3–1.

DIRECTIONS: Read through the poem as a class. Use the name of your school, if possible, or use the words "Our School" to fill in the blank. Guide students as they plan their own performance, assigning various lines to soloists, small groups, and a chorus. Encourage students to add original lines to the composition. OPTIONAL: Choreograph with newspapers for props, and action-freeze positions assumed by sections and soloists. Rehearse and perform the piece.

3–2 American Composers
American Music Week

GRADE LEVEL: 5–8

OBJECTIVE: Students will research American composers and become familiar with their works.

MATERIALS: Master 3–2

PREPARATION: Make student copies of Master 3–2. Make arrangements with media center for research time and materials for students.

DIRECTIONS: Decide whether your students will work individually or in small groups. Follow instructions on Master 3–2. Encourage students to share the results of their research with the class.

3–3 Sandwich Music
Sandwich Day, November 3

GRADE LEVEL: K–2

OBJECTIVE: Students will identify ABA form.

MATERIALS: Master 3–3; any ABA musical example (live or recorded); crayons; scissors

PREPARATION: Make student copies of Master 3–3.

DIRECTIONS: Read the top of Master 3–3 with the students. Allow time for students to color and cut out their sandwich parts. Play the ABA example, pausing between sections. Help students build their sandwiches. Play the musical example again, without pauses between parts. Instruct students to build their sandwiches as they hear the contrasting parts.

EXTENSION: Invite students to work in pairs. Combining their sandwich parts, encourage them to build a "rondo" sandwich (e.g., A B A C A).

3–4 Saxophones and Their Cousins
Saxophone Day, November 6

GRADE LEVEL: 4–6

OBJECTIVE: Students will distinguish the saxophone from other members of the woodwind family.

MATERIALS: Master 3–4; recorded examples of woodwind instruments; pictures of woodwind instruments

PREPARATION: Introduce the members of the woodwind family by sight and sound. Make multiple copies of Master 3–4. Cut apart and combine two pages of cards to create an 18-card deck for each group.

DIRECTIONS: Divide students into small groups. Give each group a deck of cards. Instruct students to shuffle cards and place them face down in the center of group. Play short excerpts of woodwind recordings. Allow time after each excerpt for each group to turn up the top card in the deck. Help the entire class agree on the woodwind instrument heard. Score one point for each group whose top card matches the correct answer. Score two points for each saxophone example. OPTIONAL: Offer a reward for the group who accumulates the most points.

EXTENSION: Invite woodwind players to visit your classroom. Invite students to write questions prior to the visit based on what they have learned about the woodwind family.

3–5, 3–6 Sempre Fidelis
John Philip Sousa, November 6

GRADE LEVEL: 1–3 (4–8)

OBJECTIVE: Students will follow a listening map, and identify sections of a Sousa march.

3–5, 3–6, Sempre Fidelis, continued

MATERIALS: Master 3–5 or 3–6; recording of John Philip Sousa's "Sempre Fidelis"

PREPARATION: Choose Master 3–5 or 3–6 as appropriate to your students' ability levels. Make a transparency and student copies of the master.

DIRECTIONS: Display transparency. Isolate and discuss the main sections and themes of this march. Play the recording in segments, following the map. Distribute student copies of Master 3–5 (3–6). Play the entire march. Invite students to follow their copies. Invite student suggestions to plan a movement or body percussion sequence that follows the form of this march. Listen to the march again and add the movement sequence.

3–7   Aaron Copland Hall of Fame
Aaron Copland, November 14

GRADE LEVEL: 4–8

OBJECTIVE: Students will use their knowledge of the life and works of Aaron Copland to create a Hall of Fame.

MATERIALS: Master 3–7; large cardboard boxes; Copland recordings; art supplies; sound equipment; headphones

PREPARATION: Study the life and works of Aaron Copland. Make copies of Master 3–7 for each group.

DIRECTIONS: Divide the class into small groups. Assign one or more of the following tasks to each group.

Build the "structure."

Create a biographical sketch for Aaron Copland.

Create a musical exhibit for the Hall of Fame. You will need many exhibits. Each exhibit may include a recorded or live performance of one of Copland's works, as well as a visual representation of the work.

Plan and set up the sound equipment, including headphones, for each exhibit.

Decorate the outside of the structure.

Create invitations and publicity for Hall of Fame Tours.

Conduct tours through the Hall of Fame.

Help the class sequence the tasks and establish deadlines for each. Instruct each group to follow instructions on Master 3–7. When each group has completed its task, invite guests to tour the Hall of Fame.

3–8 Young Person's Guide to the Orchestra
Benjamin Britten, November 22, 1913

GRADE LEVEL: 4–6

OBJECTIVE: Students will identify instruments of the orchestra.

MATERIALS: Master 3–8; recording of Benjamin Britten's "Young Person's Guide to the Orchestra"

PREPARATION: Make copies of Master 3–8. Cut cards apart to make one full 13-card set for each student or pair of students.

DIRECTIONS: Distribute card sets. Instruct students to spread their cards out face up. Play the recording (theme and variations section only). Instruct students to sequence cards as they listen. Announce correct answers during each variation. On subsequent experiences, announce correct answers after each variation, or after the entire composition is played.

ANSWER KEY: flute and piccolo, oboe, clarinet, bassoon, violin, viola, cello, double bass, harp, French horn, trumpet, trombone and tuba, percussion

3–9 Maple Leaf Rag
Scott Joplin, November 24, 1868

GRADE LEVEL: 4–8

OBJECTIVE: Students will follow a ragtime listening chart.

MATERIALS: Master 3–9; recording of Scott Joplin's "Maple Leaf Rag"

PREPARATION: Make a transparency and student copies of Master 3–9.

DIRECTIONS: Display transparency. Distribute student copies. Help students follow the 16-bar sections by pointing to the "1 2" in each measure on the chart. Invite students to do the same, and remind them to observe repeat signs. Play the entire recording and call out letter names and repeats as sections change. Replay the recording without vocal cues. Observe students' abilities to follow the chart accurately.

3–10 On the First Thanksgiving
Thanksgiving

GRADE LEVEL: 2–4

OBJECTIVE: Students will compose a pentatonic song.

3–10, On the First Thanksgiving, *continued*

MATERIALS: Master 3–10; bellsets; mallets; pencils

PREPARATION: Make student copies of Master 3–10.

DIRECTIONS: Decide whether students will work individually or in small groups. Review student directions with the class. Allow time for students to compose. Encourage students to perform their compositions for the class.

3–11 Thank You, Lord
Thanksgiving

GRADE LEVEL: 3–6

OBJECTIVE: Students will sing a round with instrumental accompaniment.

MATERIALS: Master 3–11; mallet instruments

PREPARATION: Make a transparency or student copies of Master 3–11.

DIRECTIONS: Help students learn to sing "Thank You, Lord." Add the instrumental parts one by one. Divide the class into two sections and sing the song as a round. Add the instrumental parts to the round.

3–12 Over the River and through the Wood
Thanksgiving

GRADE LEVEL: 1–3

OBJECTIVE: Students will follow a melodic contour map and perform a song.

MATERIALS: Master 3–12; bellsets

PREPARATION: Make a transparency and student copies of Master 3–12.

DIRECTIONS: Help students follow the melodic contour map as they sing the song. Help students learn to play phrase 1 and phrase 3 on bells. Add the bell parts to the song.

3–13 Turkey Shoot
Thanksgiving

GRADE LEVEL: 3–5

OBJECTIVE: Students will perform a chant with body percussion.

MATERIALS: Master 3–13

PREPARATION: Make a transparency of Master 3–13.

DIRECTIONS: Help students learn to speak the chant with correct rhythms. Divide the class into four groups. Assign one line of the body percussion to each group. Rehearse each part separately and then in sequence. Perform chant with body percussion parts added.

EXTENSION: (1) Perform the chant as a two-, three-, or four-part round with body percussion parts. (2) Sing the chant. Use the melody to "Short'nin' Bread."

Name _____   **Date** _____

3–1   # Extra! Extra! Our School Is Great!

_____ Extra! Extra! _____'s great!

_____ We're the kids who really rate.

_____ Extra! Extra! Shout out loud.

_____ We stand out in any crowd!

_____ Extra! Extra! We're the best!

_____ North, South, East, or West!

_____ From the Florida Keys to Puget Sound,

_____ Simply the finest school around.

_____ Extra! Extra-ordinary!

_____ No one here is secondary.

_____ Let us recapitulate.

_____ Extra! Extra! _____'s great!

© 1992 by Loretta Mitchell

Name _____   **Date** _____

3–2   # American Composers

Directions: Follow the steps below to research an American composer and his or her music.

1. Choose a composer. You may choose one from this list or look elsewhere for names of American composers.

   _____ Samuel Barber   _____ Leonard Bernstein   _____ Aaron Copland

   _____ Natalie Sleeth   _____ George Gershwin   _____ Morton Gould

   _____ Charles Ives   _____ Alice Parker   _____ Libby Larsen

2. Go to the library and find the answers to these questions about your composer.

   a. Composer's full name _____

   b. Date of birth _____ Date of death _____

   c. Place of birth _____

   d. One interesting fact about the composer's childhood:

      _____

   e. One interesting fact about the composer's musical training:

      _____

   f. The names of two of the composer's works:

      _____

      _____

3. Find a recording of this composer's work. Listen to the recording. Fill in the following:

   a. The title of the composition that you chose:

      _____

   b. Your reaction to your composer's music:

      _____

      _____

4. Share your research, your composer's music, and your reactions with your classmates.

Name _____ Date _____

Sandwich Music

Are you hungry? Make a sandwich. Use two slices of bread on the outside and a piece of meat or cheese on the inside.

ABA music is like a sandwich. ABA music has three parts. The first and the last parts are alike. The middle part is different.

Color and cut out the parts of your sandwich. Listen to the ABA music your teacher plays. Make your sandwich as you listen to each part.

3–4

Saxophones and Their Cousins

bassoon	saxophone	oboe
piccolo	flute	clarinet
flute	saxophone	clarinet

Name _____   Date _____

3–5

Sempre Fidelis

by John Philip Sousa

INTRODUCTION

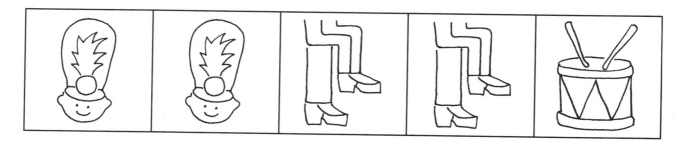

Name _____   Date _____

3–6   **Sempre Fidelis**

by John Philip Sousa

```
┌─────────────────┐
│                 │
│  INTRODUCTION   │
│                 │
└─────────────────┘
```

Theme A   Theme B

A	Á	B	B	BRIDGE

Theme C   Theme D

C	C′	C″	D	D′

Name _____ Date _____

Aaron Copland Hall of Fame

GROUP NUMBER _____ Members _____ _____ _____ _____

YOUR TASK _____ **DEADLINE** _____

PLAN
What is your plan to accomplish your task?

Step 1 _____ Step 2 _____

Step 3 _____ Step 4 _____

TIME LINE
What is your deadline? _____

How will you meet your deadline? _____

_____

MATERIALS AND EQUIPMENT

What will you need? _____ _____ _____ _____

_____ _____ _____ _____ _____

GETTING THE JOB DONE
How will you divide up the work so that each group member has a job?
When does each job have to be completed?

_____ _____ _____
name   job   deadline

_____ _____ _____
name   job   deadline

_____ _____ _____
name   job   deadline

_____ _____ _____
name   job   deadline

3–8   # Young Person's Guide to the Orchestra

by Benjamin Britten

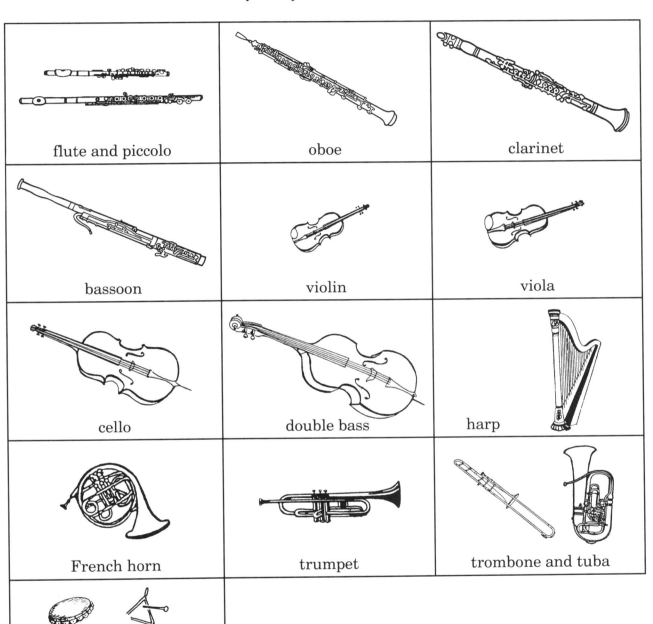

flute and piccolo	oboe	clarinet
bassoon	violin	viola
cello	double bass	harp
French horn	trumpet	trombone and tuba
percussion		

3–9

Maple Leaf Rag
by Scott Joplin

INTRODUCTION 4 measures

| 1 2 | 1 2 | 1 2 | 1 2 |

A   16 measures and repeat

| 1 2 | 1 2 | 1 2 | 1 2 | 1 2 | 1 2 | 1 2 | 1 2 |

| 1 2 | 1 2 | 1 2 | 1 2 | 1 2 | 1 2 | 1 2 | 1 2 | :‖

B   16 measures and repeat

| 1 2 | 1 2 | 1 2 | 1 2 | 1 2 | 1 2 | 1 2 | 1 2 |

| 1 2 | 1 2 | 1 2 | 1 2 | 1 2 | 1 2 | 1 2 | 1 2 | :‖

A   16 measures NO REPEAT

| 1 2 | 1 2 | 1 2 | 1 2 | 1 2 | 1 2 | 1 2 | 1 2 |

| 1 2 | 1 2 | 1 2 | 1 2 | 1 2 | 1 2 | 1 2 | 1 2 |

C   16 measures and repeat

| 1 2 | 1 2 | 1 2 | 1 2 | 1 2 | 1 2 | 1 2 | 1 2 |

| 1 2 | 1 2 | 1 2 | 1 2 | 1 2 | 1 2 | 1 2 | 1 2 | :‖

A   16 measures and repeat

| 1 2 | 1 2 | 1 2 | 1 2 | 1 2 | 1 2 | 1 2 | 1 2 |

| 1 2 | 1 2 | 1 2 | 1 2 | 1 2 | 1 2 | 1 2 | 1 2 | :‖

3–10   # On the First Thanksgiving

Directions: Compose a song for Thanksgiving. Use these bells.

C	D	E		G	A

Write one letter in each box below. Sing the words as you play. Sing your melody with verse 2.

On	the	first	Thanks- giv-		ing,

Pil -	grims	knelt	to	say,

"Thank	you,	Lord,	for	food	and	friends.

Thank	you,	Lord,	we	pray."

2. On the first Thanksgiving,
    Pilgrims knelt to say,
    "Thank you, Lord, for families,
    Thank you, Lord, we pray."

Add words to complete verse three:

3. On the first Thanksgiving,
    Pilgrims knelt to say,
    "Thank you, Lord, for _____,
    Thank you, Lord, we pray."

Name _____   **Date** _____

3–11   **Thank You, Lord**

Thank   you,   Lord.   Thank   you,   Lord.

For   food   and   drink   and   fam - i - ly.   Thank   you,   Lord.

Add these instrument parts to the round:

Alto Glockenspiel

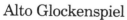

Alto Metallophone

Bass Xylophone

Instrumental accompaniments by Jane Frazee, Director, University of St. Thomas Institute for Contemporary Music Education..

Name _____ **Date** _____

3–12   **Over the River and through the Wood**

Ⓒ Grandmother's Ⓑ house Ⓐ we Ⓖ go —

Ⓖ O - ver the riv- Ⓔ er Ⓕ and Ⓖ through the wood, to

The horse knows the way to carry the sleigh through the white and drift- ed snow

Ⓒ how the Ⓑ wind Ⓐ does Ⓖ blow! —

Ⓖ O - ver the riv- Ⓔ er Ⓕ and Ⓖ through the wood, oh,

It stings the toes, and bites the nose, as o -ver the ground we go! —

Name _____   Date _____

3–13   **Turkey Shoot**

Take   out   your   mus - ket,   take   out   your   gun,

Gon - na have   a   tur - key shoot,   gon - na have   fun.

Look   to   the   tree - tops,   look   to   the   sky,

Shoot   'em   down   low   and   shoot   'em   up   high.

Ten   pound,   twen - ty   pound,   thir - ty   pound,   too,

Need   a   lot - ta   tur - key 'cuz   a   lit - tle won't   do.

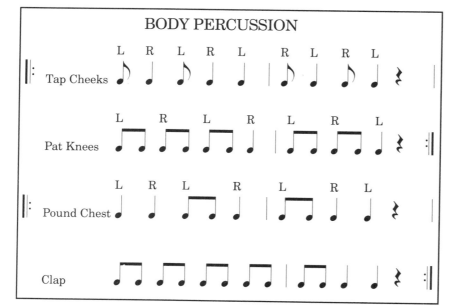

BODY PERCUSSION

Tap Cheeks   L R L R L R L R L

Pat Knees   L   R   L   R   L   R   L

Pound Chest   L R L   R   L   R   L

Clap

DECEMBER
TEACHER'S GUIDE

4–1 Unsquare Dance
Dave Brubeck, December 5

GRADE LEVEL: 4–8

OBJECTIVE: Students will analyze rhythmic and harmonic patterns and will describe jazz improvisation in "Unsquare Dance."

MATERIALS: Master 4–1; recording of Dave Brubeck's "Unsquare Dance"; resonator bells: A and G, D and C, E and D; dictionary

PREPARATION: Make student copies of Master 4–1.

DIRECTIONS: *(1) Rhythmic patterns:* Write this pattern on the board:

1 ₂ 1 ₂ 1 ₂₃

Help students clap the rhythm pattern. Play the recording of "Unsquare Dance." Help students count the pattern as they listen. Distribute student copies. Help students follow the rhythm pattern with their pencil points. Replay the recording. Help students mark the handclaps above the beats with X's.

(2) Harmonic patterns: Direct students' attention to the harmony map. Distribute resonator bells to three students. Help students practice harmonic patterns on bells. Replay the recording. Instruct bell players to play along with the recording and other students to follow their harmonic maps as they listen.

(3) Jazz improvisation: Once students are familiar with the rhythmic and harmonic structure of the piece, encourage them to listen for improvisation. Direct students' attention to Item 4. Instruct them to listen and to answer the questions. Compare answers and relisten to the piece.

4–2 Symphony No. 5
Ludwig van Beethoven, December 16

GRADE LEVEL: 4–8

OBJECTIVE: Students will play and identify a melodic motive.

MATERIALS: Master 4–2; four water glasses and one spoon for each group; pitcher of water for each group; recording of Ludwig van Beethoven's Fifth Symphony, first movement

PREPARATION: Make a copy of Master 4–2 for each group.

DIRECTIONS: Introduce Beethoven's Fifth Symphony. Divide the class into small groups. Give each group a copy of Master 4–2. Clarify instructions if necessary. Allow time for each group to work. Invite each group to perform for the class. Play the recording. Direct students' attention to this famous motive as they listen. As a class, count the number of times the motive occurs in the first movement.

4–3 Dot Dot Dot Dash
Ludwig van Beethoven, December 16

GRADE LEVEL: 4–8

OBJECTIVE: Students will use a famous musical motive as the basis for their own compositions.

MATERIALS: Master 4–3; keyboards or bellsets

PREPARATION: Make student copies of Master 4–3. Prepare students with a listening lesson focusing on the familiar motive in Beethoven's Fifth Symphony, first movement. See Activity 4–2.

DIRECTIONS: Determine whether students will work individually or in small groups. Distribute student copies. Clarify instructions and demonstrate several of the suggestions (Item 2). Allow time for students to experiment and plan their compositions. Encourage students to perform their compositions for the class.

4–4 Hanukkah
A Song for Hanukkah

GRADE LEVEL: 2–4

OBJECTIVE: Students will sequence four phrases of a song.

MATERIALS: Master 4–4

PREPARATION: Make student copies of Master 4–4. Cut strips apart. Separate sets of strips into syllable strips and traditional notation strips.

DIRECTIONS: Distribute sets of syllable strips. Sing the first phrase of the song on a neutral syllable. Invite students to find a strip to match the melody they heard. Continue with other phrases. When students have strips in the correct order, sing each phrase with the lyrics instead of a neutral syllable. Invite students to sing the song with you. Distribute traditional notation strips. Instruct students to match each strip to a corresponding syllable strip. Once strips are sequenced and matched, help students determine the form of the song. Label each strip with a picture or a letter.

ANSWER KEY: AA´ AB or pictures in same sequence.

4–5 Violins and How They Work
Antonio Stradivari, December 18

GRADE LEVEL: 2–5

OBJECTIVE: Students will identify the major parts of a violin.

MATERIALS: Master 4–5; violin or picture of a violin; recording of a violin solo

PREPARATION: Make student copies of Master 4–5.

DIRECTIONS: Play the recording to introduce the sound of the violin. Display the picture or the violin. Discuss the way it makes sounds. Distribute student copies of Master 4–5. Allow time for students to work. Compare and correct answers. Replay the violin recording.

4–6 Build Your Own String Instrument
Antonio Stradivari, December 18

GRADE LEVEL: 5–8

OBJECTIVE: Students will create an instrument that includes a bridge, a sound box, strings, and tuning pegs.

MATERIALS: Master 4–6

PREPARATION: See Activity 4–5. Make student copies of Master 4–6.

DIRECTIONS: Assign as a project for individual students, partners, or small groups. Clarify instructions if necessary. Set three due dates: one for instrument plans, one for completed instruments, and one for demonstrations. Offer your assistance in all phases of the project.

4–7 Holiday Rhythms

GRADE LEVEL: 1–8

OBJECTIVE: Students will write rhythm patterns from dictation.

MATERIALS: Master 4–7; one rhythm instrument (for example, triangle)

PREPARATION: Prepare six rhythm patterns of appropriate difficulty. Make student copies of Master 4–7.

DIRECTIONS: Distribute student copies of Master 4–12. Play rhythm patterns on a rhythm instrument. Allow time after each pattern for students to write the pattern they hear. To adapt this activity for any grade level, vary the difficulty of the patterns by length and by rhythmic content. Younger students may write patterns in icons, stick notation, or other nontraditional form as appropriate for their abilities.

4–8 Christmas Carol Challenge

GRADE LEVEL: 3–8

OBJECTIVE: Students will sing and identify familiar Christmas carols.

MATERIALS: Master 4–8; bingo chips or markers

PREPARATION: Make student copies of Master 4–8.

DIRECTIONS: Invite students to help you list on the board as many Christmas carols as possible. Distribute student copies of Master 4–8. Instruct students to choose carols from the list and write them in the grid spaces on their copies, in any order, repeating any titles as often as they wish or omitting any titles that they wish. The game is played much like bingo. Choose one student to hum (or sing on a neutral syllable) the first phrase of any Christmas carol. Class members will identify the carol and, if that carol appears on their grid, will mark their grids with bingo chips. Continue with other volunteers singing or humming Christmas carols. The object of the game is to correctly identify five tunes across, down, or diagonally.

4–9, 4–10 Jingle Bells

GRADE LEVEL: K–2

OBJECTIVE: Students will describe the verse-refrain form of a song.

MATERIALS: Masters 4–9, 4–10; wrist bells

PREPARATION: Make one copy of Master 4–9. Cut verse and refrain cards apart. Make a transparency and student copies of Master 4–10.

DIRECTIONS: Teach or review the song by rote. Hold up the verse and refrain cards and instruct the students to sit when they sing the verse and stand when they sing the refrain. Display Transparency 4–10. Ask the class to sing the verse. Trace the melodic contour shapes. Invite students to draw similar shapes in the air. Distribute student copies of Master 4–10. Invite students to trace the melody as they sing the verse again. Ask the class to sing the refrain. Follow the icons as they sing. Invite the class to use their copies and touch the icons as they sing the refrain again. Finally, invent a movement sequence to describe the form of this song. For the verse, invite students to draw the melodic contour in the air. For the refrain, invite students to create their own dance. Add wrist bells to the refrain sections.

4–11 Hallelujah Chorus

GRADE LEVEL: 4–7

OBJECTIVE: Students will identify musical motives in the "Hallelujah Chorus."

4–11, Hallelujah Chorus, continued

MATERIALS: Masters 4–11; recording of George Frederic Handel's "Hallelujah Chorus"; scissors

PREPARATION: Make student copies of Master 4–11.

DIRECTIONS: Distribute student copies. Instruct students to cut apart motive cards. Using the cards as visual aids, introduce each musical idea. Discuss the rhythmic and melodic characteristics of each idea and possible ways that it might be varied. Instruct students to arrange cards so that all are visible and to select cards as they hear each theme. Play the recording. Assist students by holding up appropriate cards. Allow students to repeat the activity without your assistance. Note: These motive cards illustrate general musical ideas only. They should not be interpreted literally for pitch or rhythmic content. You may wish to create additional, more specific cards to expand the set.

4–12 Variations on a Familiar Carol

GRADE LEVEL: 4–8

OBJECTIVE: Students will create variations on a theme.

MATERIALS: Master 4–12

PREPARATION: Make student copies of Master 4–12.

DIRECTIONS: Introduce or review the concept "Theme and Variations" (see Activity 5–10). Distribute copies of Master 4–12. Sing "We Wish You a Merry Christmas." Experiment with the sample variations suggested. Invite students to suggest additional ideas for variations. Divide the class into small groups. Allow time for groups to create their own variations. Invite groups to share their work with the class.

4–13 The Story of the Nutcracker

GRADE LEVEL: 3–5

OBJECTIVE: Students will dramatize the story of the Nutcracker.

MATERIALS: Master 4–13; recording of Peter Ilyich Tchaikovsky's "The Nutcracker"

PREPARATION: Make student copies of Master 4–13.

DIRECTIONS: Distribute student copies. Select students to read each part. Read through the play. Use this activity to introduce the music from the ballet, or select portions of the music to use during your performance. You may wish to rehearse and perform the play with costumes, scenery, and props.

Name _____   **Date** _____

4–1   # Unsquare Dance*

by Dave Brubeck

1. Listen to the rhythm pattern of "Unsquare Dance." Follow this pattern of two's and three's with your pencil point. Count "1, 2; 1, 2; 1, 2, 3" as you follow.

$$1_2 \; 1_2 \; 1_{2 \; 3}$$

Repeat this pattern.

2. Listen again. Mark an X above each beat where you hear a clap.

3. Listen for the harmony. Follow this harmonic pattern with your pencil point. Play this pattern on bells.

A	G	A
A	G	A
D	C	D
A	G	A
E	D	E
A	G	A

Repeat this pattern.

4. Listen for improvisation. Answer these questions: _____

   a. What instruments do you hear playing? _____

   _____

   b. Look up the word *improvisation*. Write its definition here: _____

   _____

   c. Choose one instrument that you hear. Describe its improvisation.

   Instrument: _____   The musician improvised like this: _____

   _____

   _____

4–2   # Symphony No. 5

by Ludwig van Beethoven

1. Tune four water glasses.

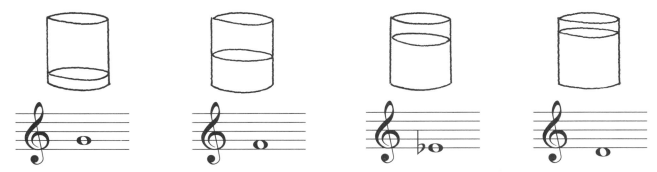

2. Play this motive on your water glasses.

3. Listen to the first movement of Beethoven's Fifth Symphony. Count the number of times you hear this famous musical motive. Mark a / in the space for each occurrence.

4. Compare your number of slashes with other class members. Listen to the first movement again to check your counting.

Name _____ Date _____

4–3   **Dot Dot Dot Dash**

Beethoven wrote a famous symphony based upon four notes. Here's your chance to compose with a famous pattern.

Directions:

1. Play this four-note motive on a keyboard or a bellset.

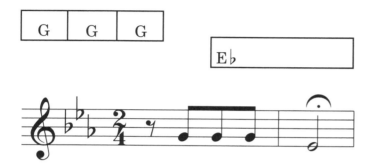

2. Experiment with the four notes.
   a. Start on a higher note.
   b. Start on a lower note.
   c. Play the notes faster.
   d. Play the notes slower.
   e. Change the pattern of highs and lows.

3. Now use your imagination to create your own musical piece based on these four notes. Play your composition. Write your ideas in the spaces below. Write your composition on the back of this page. Rehearse and perform your musical piece.

   I will introduce my composition by _____ .

   My first idea will be _____ .

   My second idea will be _____ .

   I will repeat this idea _____ .

   I will end my composition by _____ .

Name _____   Date _____

4–4   **Hanukkah**

☐	do'
	        ti
	              la ——
	sol sol — sol sol — sol
	     mi mi mi

☐	ti
	        la
	              sol ——
	fa fa — fa fa — fa
	    re re re

☐	do'
	        ti
	              la ——
	sol sol — sol sol — sol
	     mi mi mi

☐	ti ti ti — ti ti ti — ti ti do'——
	                                                 la
	                                          sol

(continued)

© 1992 by Loretta Mitchell

Name _____ **Date** _____

4–4, Hanukkah, continued

Ha - nuk - kah, Ha - nuk - kah, time to cel - e - brate.

Ha - nuk - kah, Ha - nuk - kah, Can - dles num - ber eight.

Ha - nuk - kah, Ha - nuk - kah, spe - cial games to play.

Chil - dren smile, all the while, Hap - py Hol - i - day!

Name _____ Date _____

Violins and How They Work

Directions: Write these violin terms in the correct boxes. Draw a line from each term to its place on the violin.

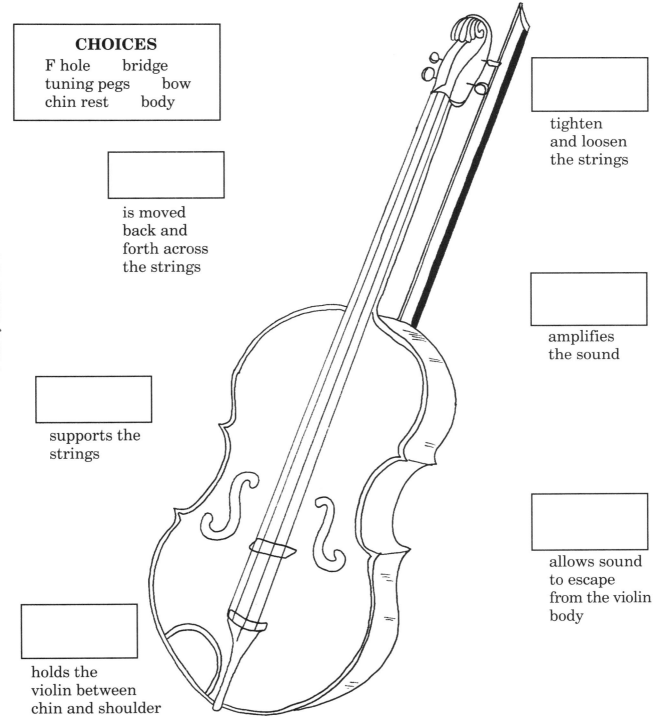

CHOICES
F hole   bridge
tuning pegs   bow
chin rest   body

tighten
and loosen
the strings

is moved
back and
forth across
the strings

amplifies
the sound

supports the
strings

allows sound
to escape
from the violin
body

holds the
violin between
chin and shoulder

© 1992 by Loretta Mitchell

Name _____   Date _____

4–6   **Build Your Own String Instrument**

Directions: Build your own string instrument. It must have a sound box, a bridge, three or four strings, and tuning pegs.

PLAN YOUR INSTRUMENT: Plans are due: _____

1. How will you play it?   _____ with a bow

     _____ by strumming the strings

     _____ by plucking the strings

     _____ other:

2. Sketch your instrument here. Label the sound box, the bridge, the strings, and the tuning pegs.

3. What will you need to build it?

_____   _____

_____   _____

_____   _____

4. What will you name your instrument? _____

BUILD YOUR INSTRUMENT:
     Your completed instrument will be due on _____ .

DEMONSTRATE YOUR INSTRUMENT:
     Your demonstration is scheduled for _____ .

4–7   **Holiday Rhythms**

1.

2.

3.

4.

5.

6.

4–8   **Christmas Carol Challenge**

		FREE		

Name _____ Date _____

4–9   **Jingle Bells**

VERSE

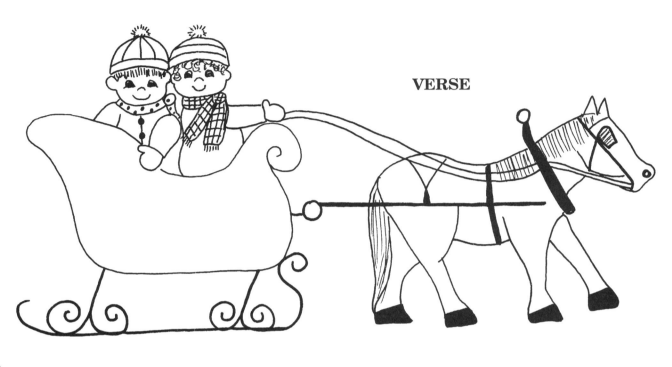

REFRAIN

4–10   **Jingle Bells**

VERSE

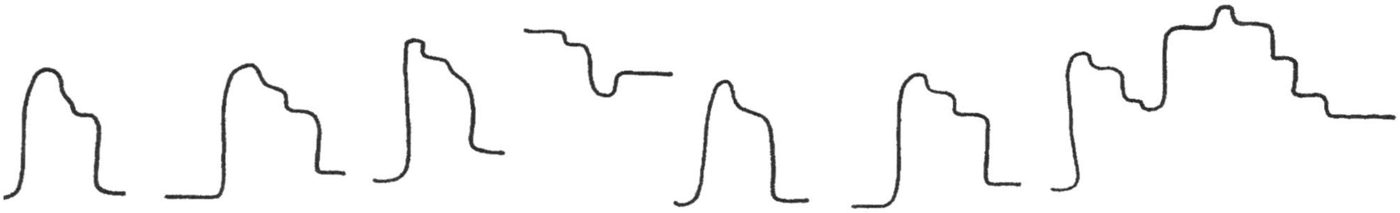

REFRAIN

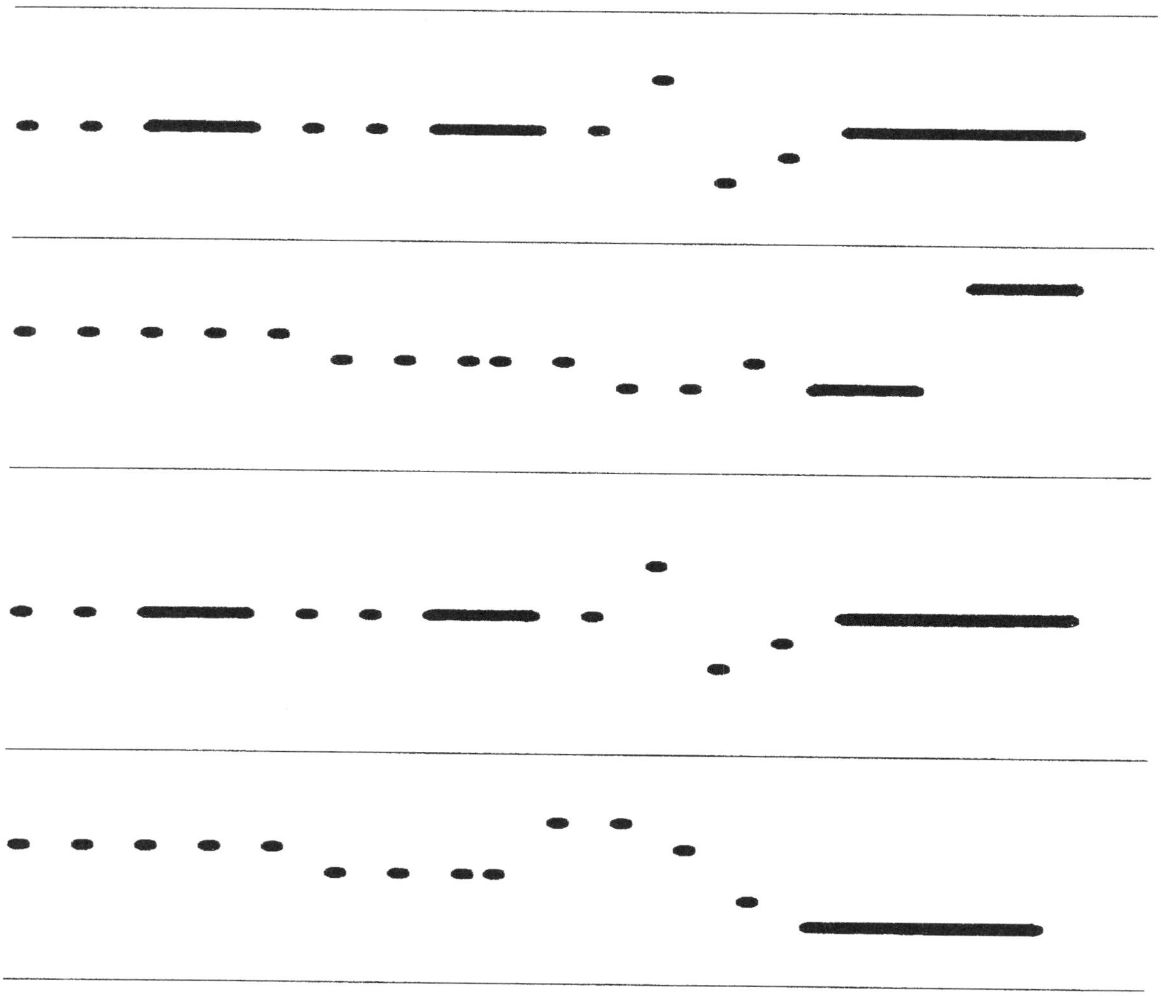

Name _____   Date _____

Hallelujah Chorus
by George Frederic Handel

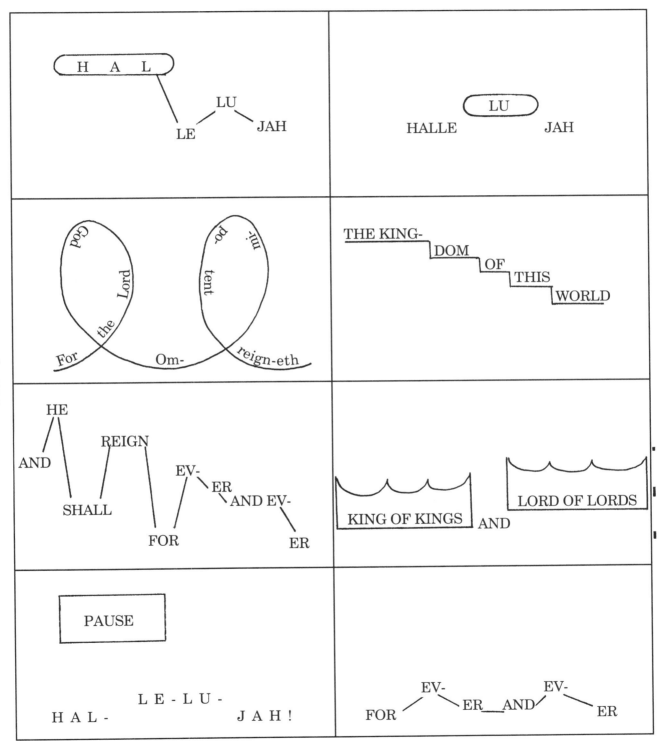

4–12   **Variations on a Familiar Carol**

1. Sing this song.

We   wish you a Mer-ry Christ-mas, We wish you a Mer-ry Christ-mas.

We   wish you a Mer-ry Christ-mas, and a Hap-py New   Year.

2. Try these ideas to create variations on the theme:
   a. Sing each syllable two times ("We we wish wish you you a a . . .").
   b. Sing the song in a minor key.
   c. Sing the song in a neutral syllable ("loo, loo, loo . . .").
   d. Add a hand drum to accompany the song.

3. Make up seven variations of your own.

4. Choose four variations that you like the best. Create a performance plan and write it here. Perform your theme and variations for the class.

<u>Theme</u>   <u>We Wish You a Merry Christmas</u>

VARIATION 1   _____

VARIATION 2   _____

VARIATION 3   _____

VARIATION 4   _____

Name _____   Date _____

4–13   **The Story of the Nutcracker**

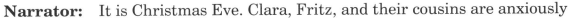

Setting: Christmas Eve many years ago,
Clara and Fritz's home. Christmas tree
is in center of stage.

Characters: Narrator
Clara
Fritz
Godfather
Cousins: Thomas, Maria, and Angela
Mice
Nutcracker Prince

Narrator: It is Christmas Eve. Clara, Fritz, and their cousins are anxiously waiting for Godfather to arrive.

Clara: I wish Godfather would hurry.

Fritz: There's the door. (*Running to the door*) I'll get it!

Clara: (*Running after him*) No, let's both go!

Godfather: Merry Christmas, children, Merry Christmas to you all!

Clara: Come on in! We're so glad you're here!

Fritz: (*To the other children*) Oh! Look how many presents he's carrying!

Cousins: (*Running to the door*) Godfather! Godfather! What did you bring us?

Godfather: (*Coming through the door*) Now just hold on, children. I have plenty of presents for everyone. Let me get my coat off.

Narrator: Clara and Fritz help Godfather take off his coat. The cousins help Godfather place the presents under the tree.

Godfather: Now let's see. I have this present for Thomas. This one is for Maria. And here is one for Angela. This one is for Fritz. And this last one . . . a very special gift for my Godchild, Clara.

Narrator: The children open their presents and thank Godfather. Clara says nothing. She stares in amazement at the beautiful gift she receives!

Godfather: Well, Clara, don't you like it?

4–13, The Story of the Nutcracker, continued

Clara: It's . . . it's . . . it's the most beautiful present I've ever seen! Oh, thank you, Godfather. Thank you ever so much!

Godfather: You're more than welcome, my dear child. Now have a good time with your nutcracker.

Fritz: Let me see that thing!

Narrator: Fritz grabs the nutcracker from Clara. The head of the nutcracker falls off.

Clara: (*Crying*) Oh, Fritz! Now see what you've done. It's broken, and it will never be the same.

Godfather: There, there, my dear. It can be fixed.

Narrator: Godfather takes a handkerchief from his pocket. He ties it around the broken nutcracker and places it in the doll cradle.

Godfather: He'll be well by morning. Now, all of you, it's time for bed. Get your things, it's time to go.

Cousins: Goodnight! Thank you for the presents, Godfather!

Godfather: You're welcome, and Merry Christmas.

Narrator: And so the cousins leave to go to bed.

Godfather: Clara and Fritz, it's your bedtime too.

Clara and Fritz: Very well, Godfather. Good night. Thank you for the presents.

Narrator: So Clara and Fritz go off to bed as well. But a magical night is just beginning. Clara cannot sleep, so she creeps back down to the living room. She sees life-size mice attacking the toys under the tree and the nutcracker coming to life to help defend the toys.

Nutcracker: Oh, no you don't, you mice! We toys are stronger than you may think!

Mouse 1: Take that!

Narrator: The mouse strikes at the nutcracker with his sword! The battle continues. The nutcracker's life is in danger. Clara takes off her slipper, throws it at the mouse, and saves the nutcracker's life.

Nutcracker: Oh, Clara! How can I ever thank you! You must come with me to the Land of Sweets. I would like you to be my guest for a party in your honor!

Narrator: A magical candy sleigh appears. Clara and the Nutcracker Prince step into the sleigh and fly away to the Land of Sweets for a make-believe evening Clara will never forget!

THE END

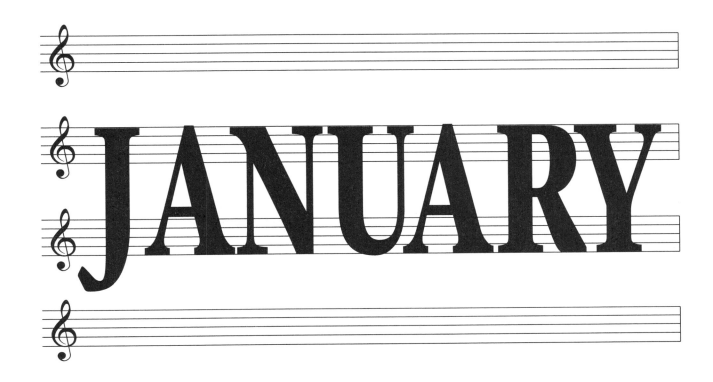

JANUARY
TEACHER'S GUIDE

5–1 A Song for the New Year

GRADE LEVEL: 5–8

OBJECTIVE: Students will rewrite song lyrics.

MATERIALS: Master 5–1

PREPARATION: Make student copies of Master 5–1.

DIRECTIONS: Sing "Auld Lang Syne" with the class. Discuss its common use at New Year's celebrations. Clarify directions if necessary. Allow time for students to work. Invite students to perform their lyrics for the class.

5–2 New Year's Chords

GRADE LEVEL: 3–6

OBJECTIVE: Students will play chords to accompany a song.

MATERIALS: Master 5–2; resonator bells; mallets

PREPARATION: Make a transparency or student copies of Master 5–2.

DIRECTIONS: Distribute F, A, and C bells to three students; C, E, G, and B♭ bells to three students; and B♭, D, and F bells to three students. Invite each chord group to play a tremolo together. Continue the lesson by following the directions on Master 5–2. Add the bell chord groups to the song.

5–3 Music Trivia
Trivia Day, January 4

GRADE LEVEL: 5–8

OBJECTIVE: Students will write and answer music trivia questions.

MATERIALS: Master 5–3

PREPARATION: Make two copies of Master 5–3 for each group. Arrange for students to visit the library or locate reference books and research materials for student use.

DIRECTIONS: Divide the class into small groups. Instruct groups to follow the instructions on Master 5–3, to research their questions, and to write

answers for them. When all groups have turned in two copies of their questions (and answers), distribute questions and begin Task 2.
OPTIONAL: Offer a prize to the group with the most correct answers.

5–4 Contrasts
Elvis Presley, January 8

GRADE LEVEL: 5–8

OBJECTIVE: Students will compare musical elements of two Elvis Presley hits.

MATERIALS: Master 5–4; recordings of two Elvis Presley hits

PREPARATION: Make a transparency and student copies of Master 5–4. Select (or allow students to select) two songs to compare and contrast.

DIRECTIONS: Review musical elements with the class. Introduce both musical examples. Encourage discussion about the use of musical elements to create contrasting musical moods. Instruct students to complete the grid as they listen individually and follow with class discussion. Or complete the grid as a class, working through one musical element at a time. Relisten to each musical example as many times as necessary.

5–5 Martin
Martin Luther King Day, Third Monday of January

GRADE LEVEL: 4–6

OBJECTIVE: Students will improvise melodies and create a rondo.

MATERIALS: Master 5–5; chord instrument (for example, guitar, autoharp, keyboard)

PREPARATION: Make one copy of Master 5–5.

DIRECTIONS: Help students learn Part A. Accompany Part A with chords as indicated. Demonstrate melodic improvisation for Parts B, C, and/or D. Encourage volunteers to improvise melodies for each part. Select one performer for each part. Assemble a rondo as follows: Part A (class), Part B (solo), Part A (class), Part C (solo), Part A (class), Part D (solo), Part A (class).

5–6 Pizza for All
National Pizza Week

GRADE LEVEL: 3–6

OBJECTIVE: Students will perform a speech canon with accompaniment.

MATERIALS: Master 5–6

5–6, Pizza for All, continued

PREPARATION: Make a transparency of Master 5–6.

DIRECTIONS: Help students learn the rhyme. Perform it as a canon in two, three, or four parts. Add body percussion as indicated on Master 5–6. Add instruments as indicated. Add the ostinato. Perform the canon with body percussion, instruments, and ostinato.

5–7 Figure Eight Forms

GRADE LEVEL: 4–6

OBJECTIVE: Students will find examples of musical forms.

MATERIALS: Master 5–7; music textbooks

PREPARATION: Make a transparency of Master 5–7.

DIRECTIONS: Display transparency. Review each musical form with students. Challenge students to find one or more examples of each form in their music books. Sing or listen to each example as it is suggested. As the class agrees upon appropriate examples of each, select a student to write the song title in each space on the transparency.

5–8 Symphony No. 40
Wolfgang Amadeus Mozart, January 27

GRADE LEVEL: 3–6

OBJECTIVE: Students will identify occurrences of two musical themes in a listening example.

MATERIALS: Master 5–8; bellsets or keyboards; recording of Wolfgang Amadeus Mozart's Symphony No. 40, first movement

PREPARATION: Make student copies of Master 5–8. Write this pattern on the board:

Clap and speak the pattern. Choose vocal syllables for the short and long icons (for example, "short short long" or "ti ti ta.")

DIRECTIONS: Distribute student copies. Help students compare the rhythm of the "short short long" pattern with the rhythm of Theme A. Invite students to sing the "short short long" pattern as you play. Allow time for students to learn to play Theme A. Compare the icons to the traditional notation. Play the beginning of the first movement of Symphony No. 40. Encourage students to trace the Theme A icons as they hear Theme A. Direct students' attention to Theme B. Discuss the singing, smooth quality of this theme. Invite students to trace the icons as you sing the theme. Play the exposition section of the first movement. Invite students to trace icons for Theme A and Theme B as they listen. Play the entire first movement. Help students identify Theme A, Theme B, and their variations as they listen.

5–9   Doo Dah, Doo Dah
Stephen Foster Memorial Day, January 13

GRADE LEVEL: 5–8

OBJECTIVE: Students will identify and sequence phrases from two Stephen Foster songs.

MATERIALS: Master 5–9; recordings of "Camptown Races" and "Oh! Susanna" (optional); scissors

PREPARATION: Make student copies of Master 5–9. Sing "Camptown Races" and "Oh! Susanna."

DIRECTIONS: Distribute student copies of Master 5–9. Instruct students to (a) cut apart the melody blocks, (b) mix and shuffle the blocks from both songs, (c) separate phrases that belong to "Camptown Races" from phrases that belong to "Oh! Susanna," and (d) sequence the blocks for each song. Sing each song (or play recordings) as many times as necessary to help students complete all three tasks. Compare and correct answers. Instruct students to sing both songs again, following their sets of sequenced melody blocks.

5–10, 5–11   The Trout
Franz Schubert, January 31

GRADE LEVEL: 4–6

OBJECTIVE: Students will describe theme and variations form.

MATERIALS: Masters 5–10, 5–11; recording of Franz Schubert's Piano Quintet in A Major, fourth movement; crayons, markers, pencils

PREPARATION: Make student copies of Masters 5–10 and 5–11.

DIRECTIONS: Distribute student copies of Master 5–10. Help students follow the directions, fill in the variations grid, and create graphic fish variations. Discuss the concept of "Theme and Variations" in a musical context. Distribute student copies of Master 5–11. Sing or play the theme. Invite students to follow the notation and sing along. Play the recording and call out numbers to identify each variation as it occurs. Instruct students to follow the page directions. Allow students several opportunities to hear the recording.

5–10, 5–11, The Trout, continued

ANSWER KEY: Variation 1: piano with trills; Variation 2: violin countermelody; Variation 3: bass and cello play theme, piano countermelody; Variation 4: piano and strings, minor, *f*; Variation 5: cello, slower, legato; Variation 6: cello and violin alternate

5–12, 5–13 Gunpowder Run

GRADE LEVEL: 4–6

OBJECTIVE: Students will review music theory terms and symbols.

MATERIALS: Masters 5–12, 5–13; flash cards or pictures of music symbols; two game tokens of different shapes; one pair of dice

PREPARATION: Make a transparency of Master 5–12. Make one copy of Master 5–13 on heavy paper or tagboard. Cut apart the cards.

DIRECTIONS: Display transparency. Place Ski Shop cards face down on the transparency. Divide class into two ski teams and assign each team a game token. Instruct students to take turns naming, identifying, or defining music symbols and terms. For each correct answer, a player moves the token ahead one space. A player who lands on a striped square draws a card from the Ski Shop and follows instructions on the card. A player who lands on a mitten space shakes the dice. If doubles appear, the player moves ahead to the next mitten space. The first team to reach the chalet at the bottom of the mountain wins.

Name _____ **Date** _____

5–1   **A Song for the New Year**

Directions:

1. Look up these words in the dictionary. Write the definition and origin of each word.

AULD _____   _____
                definition   origin

LANG SYNE _____   _____
                definition   origin

2. Sing the song.

Auld Lang Syne
Old Scottish Air

Should auld ac - quain - tance be for - got,

And nev - er brought to mind.

Should auld ac - quain - tance be for - got,

In days of auld lang syne.

3. Discuss the meaning of the lyrics. Why is this a good New Year's song?

4. On the back of this page, rewrite the words to "Auld Lang Syne." Be sure to keep the original meaning. Use words, phrases, and expressions that you and your friends might use in everyday conversation. Sing your words with the original melody.

Name _____   Date _____

New Year's Chords

Directions:

1. Distribute these bells. Divide your class into these chord groups:

F	C7	B♭
F A C	C E G B♭	B♭ D F

2. Sing this song. Use chord groups to accompany the song.

```
      C                                   B♭
      A                                   G
      F                                   E
                                          C
Should  auld        ac – quain – tance    be        for – got,

      C                             F
      A                             D
      F                             B♭
And    ne – ver      brought   to   mind

      C                                   B♭
      A                                   G
      F                                   E
                                          C
Should  auld        ac – quain – tance    be        for – got,

      F                    B♭                C
      D                    G                 A
      B♭                   E                 F
                          C
In      days        of         auld    lang   syne.
```

Name _____   Date _____

5–3   **Music Trivia**

Directions:
TASK 1: Each group member will write one music trivia question. Make two copies of
your questions. Write the correct answers on one copy only. Give both copies
to your teacher.
TASK 2: Each group member will answer one question written by another group. Give
your answers to your teacher.

1. Write a question about a music composer.

_____

_____   Written by: _____

Answer: _____   Answered by: _____

2. Write a question about a famous performer.

_____

_____   Written by: _____

Answer: _____   Answered by: _____

3. Write a question about a musical instrument.

_____

_____   Written by: _____

Answer: _____   Answered by: _____

4. Write a question about a famous song or musical composition.

_____

_____   Written by: _____

Answer: _____   Answered by: _____

Name _____   **Date** _____

5–4   **Contrasts**

Directions: Choose two of Elvis Presley's hits. Write their titles in the spaces below. Listen carefully to both hits. Compare and contrast their musical elements. Write your discoveries in the chart below.

	Hit #1 _____	Hit #2 _____
Rhythm		
Melody		
Harmony		
Form		
Articulation		
Tempo		
Dynamics		
Musical effect or mood		

Name _____   **Date** _____

5–5   **Martin**

Part A:

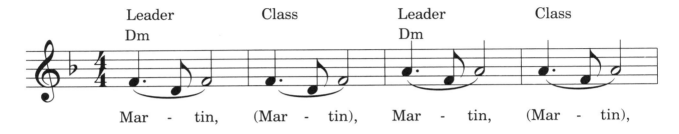

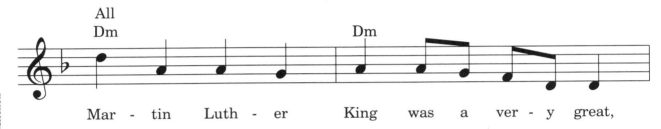

Part B: A great man who had a dream.

Part C: A great man who dreamed of brotherhood.

Part D: A great man who worked for his dream: equality for all.

Name _____ **Date** _____

5–6 **Pizza for All**

1. Learn a rhyme. Perform it as a canon.

(1)

Piz - za   par - lor   piz - za   please,

(2)

Topped   with   moz - za - rel - la   cheese.

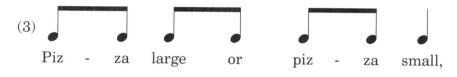

(3)

Piz - za   large   or   piz - za   small,

(4)

Piz - za   must   be   good   for   all.

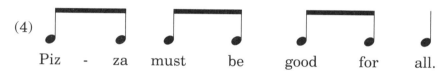

2. Add body percussion:
   Line 1: stamp   Line 2:   pat knees
   Line 3: clap   Line 4:   snap fingers

3. Add instruments:
   "please"—triangle
   "cheese"—tambourine
   "large"—glockenspiel glissando up
   "small"—glockenspiel glissando down
   "Pizza must be good for all." tone block

4. Add an ostinato:

"Piz - za must   be good   for all."

5. Perform a canon with body percussion, instruments, and ostinato.

5–7   **Figure Eight Forms**

1.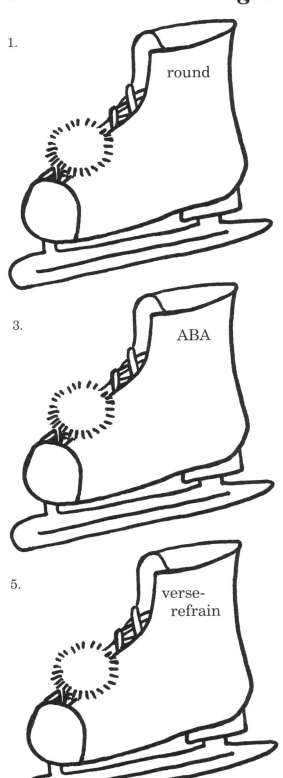
round

2.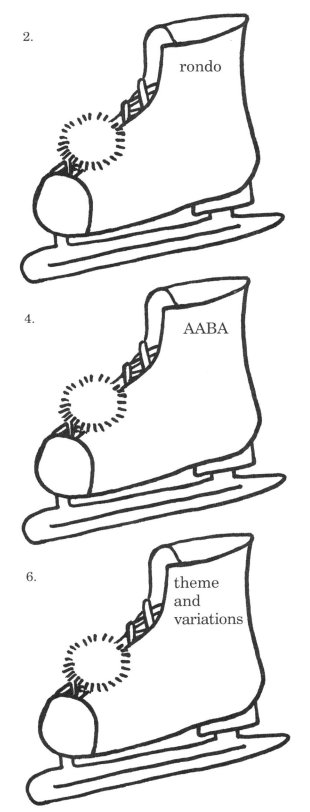
rondo

3. ABA

4. AABA

5. verse-refrain

6. theme and variations

Name _____   Date _____

5–8

Symphony No. 40

by Wolfgang Amadeus Mozart

Theme A

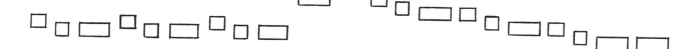

This is how Mozart wrote Theme A:

Theme B

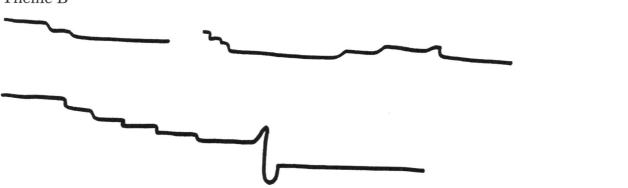

This is how Mozart wrote Theme B:

Listen to the exposition section of this movement. Trace Theme A and Theme B every time you hear them.

Name _____

Date _____

5–9

Doo Dah, Doo Dah

Directions: Sing "Camptown Races" and "Oh! Susanna." Draw each melody in the air as you sing. Cut these melody blocks apart. Decide which blocks belong to "Camptown Races" and which blocks belong to "Oh! Susanna." Arrange the blocks for each song in the correct order, and sing each song again. Follow your melody blocks as you sing.

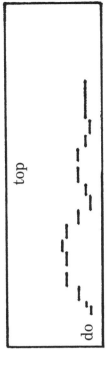

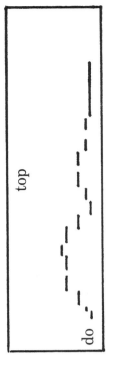

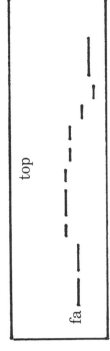

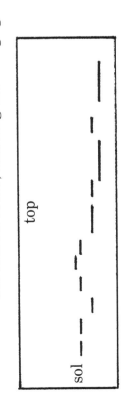

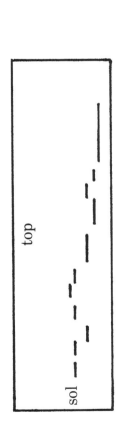

Name _____   Date _____

Theme and Variations

Find variations on the following themes. Complete this grid.

Theme	Variations
snacks	fruit, popcorn, cheese, chips, crackers
pets	
cars	

Fish have many different shapes, sizes, colors, and textures. Create four fish and decorate each to create variations on a fish theme.

YOUR THEME: FISH

VARIATION 1	VARIATION 2
VARIATION 3	**VARIATION 4**

5–11   # The Trout

by Franz Schubert

Directions: This is a theme composed by Schubert. Sing or play this theme.

Listen to Piano Quintet in A Major (*The Trout*) by Schubert. You will hear the theme more than once. As you listen, find a description of each variation to match what you are hearing. Label each fish with the correct variation number.

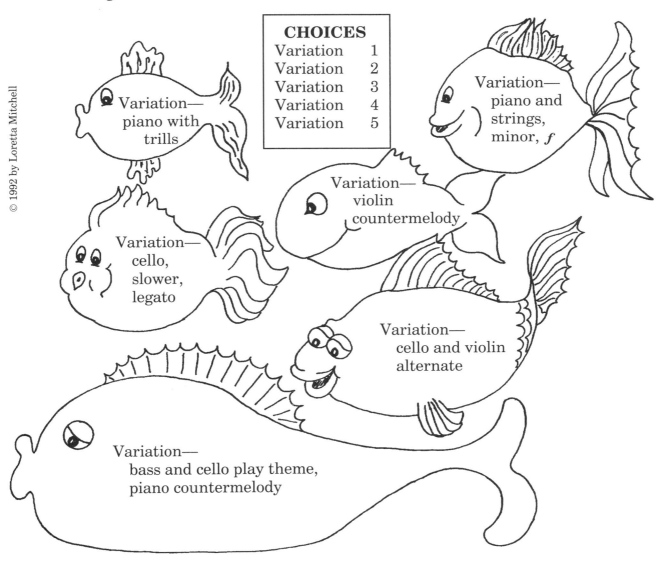

CHOICES

Variation 1
Variation 2
Variation 3
Variation 4
Variation 5

Variation—piano with trills

Variation—piano and strings, minor, *f*

Variation—violin countermelody

Variation—cello, slower, legato

Variation—cello and violin alternate

Variation—bass and cello play theme, piano countermelody

Name _____   Date _____

5–12   **Gunpowder Run**

5–13   **Gunpowder Run**

Directions: Cut apart these game cards. Shuffle the cards and place them face down on the Ski Shop space.

Lose a mitten. Go back two spaces.	You forgot how to use a chairlift! Go back three spaces.	Great turns! Take an extra turn.
Ski patrol rescues you. Advance one space.	Help a four-year-old with boots and bindings. Take an extra turn.	You missed that tree by just inches! Skip one turn to catch your breath.
Break an ankle! Lose two turns.	Fall off T-bar! Lose one turn.	New ski equipment! Move ahead one space.
Meet a new friend on the slopes. Move ahead one space.	Brave enough to try Gunpowder Run! Shake dice. If doubles, you win the game!	Practice for hours on the bunny hill. What perseverance! Move ahead one space.
Break a binding. Go back two spaces.	Lose your lift ticket. Go back four spaces.	A hole in your mitten. Go back one space.
Beautiful weather for skiing! Move ahead one space.	Lost in an avalanche! Lose two turns!	Trouble with a rope tow. Go back one space.

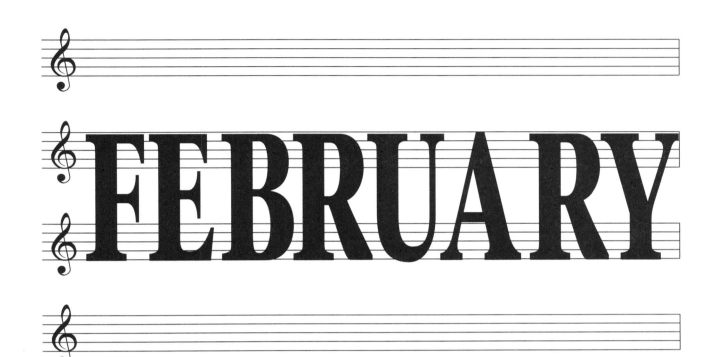

FEBRUARY
TEACHER'S GUIDE

6-1 Take Care of Your Grin
Dental Health Month

GRADE LEVEL: 2–3

OBJECTIVE: Students will compose a pentatonic song.

MATERIALS: Master 6–1; bellsets; mallets; pencils

PREPARATION: Make student copies of Master 6–1.

DIRECTIONS: Decide whether students will work individually or in small groups. Clarify instructions if necessary. Allow time for students to compose. Encourage students to perform their compositions for the class. Accompany student compositions with the following:

6-2 Will We Have More Winter?
Groundhog Day, February 2

GRADE LEVEL: 2–4

OBJECTIVE: Students will transpose a song.

MATERIALS: Master 6–2; resonator bells; mallets

PREPARATION: Make a transparency of Master 6–2.

DIRECTIONS: Teach song by rote. Sing with lyrics and syllables. Distribute resonator bells and mallets to six students. Invite class to help label each bell with a syllable name. Play and sing the song. Collect the bells. Distribute and label a second set of bells. Follow the instructions on Master 6–2 to transpose the song.

6–3 Invent a Musical Instrument
National Inventors Day, February 11

GRADE LEVEL: 4–8

OBJECTIVE: Students will design and build a musical instrument.

MATERIALS: Master 6–3

PREPARATION: Make student copies of Master 6–3. Discuss various ways that sound can be produced. Demonstrate wind, percussion, string, and electronic instruments.

DIRECTIONS: Assign as a project for individual students, partners, or small groups. Clarify instructions if necessary. Set three due dates: one for instrument plans, one for completed instruments, and one for demonstrations. Offer your assistance in all phases of the project.

6–4, 6–5 Love to Me, Love to You
Valentine's Day, February 14

GRADE LEVEL: 3–4

OBJECTIVE: Students will play a rhythm game.

MATERIALS: Masters 6–4, 6–5; chalkboard eraser; one die

PREPARATION: Make a transparency of Master 6–4. Make one copy of Master 6–5 on heavy paper or tagboard. Color hearts and cut out.

DIRECTIONS: Display transparency. Help students chant the rhyme. Begin the game by chanting the rhyme as students pass the eraser around the classroom. At the end of verse one, stop and give heart No. 1 to the child holding the eraser. Continue with verse two and heart No. 2. When all six hearts have been distributed, pause to roll the die. The child holding the lucky numbered heart becomes the leader (the person who will pass out hearts). Collect the hearts. Begin the game again.

6–6 Love Somebody
Valentine's Day, February 14

GRADE LEVEL: 1–3

OBJECTIVE: Students will label melodic icons with syllables. Students will identify matching melodic patterns. Students will read and play a melody.

6–6, Love Somebody, continued

MATERIALS: Masters 6–6, 6–7; bells or keyboard

PREPARATION: Make one copy of Master 6–7. Make a transparency and student copies of Master 6–6.

DIRECTIONS: Teach "Love Somebody" (Master 6–7) by rote. Display transparency of Master 6–6. Follow the icons as students sing the song. Distribute student copies. Sing one phrase at a time in syllables. Instruct students to fill in syllable names. Analyze each phrase for its melodic contour. Draw a shape in each box to illustrate the form of this song. Allow time for students to play the song on bells or keyboard.

ANSWER KEY: 1. *Triangle*; do mi sol sol re mi fa.
2. *Different triangle*; do mi sol sol fa mi re.
3. *Triangle*; do mi sol sol re mi fa.
4. *Circle or square*; mi mi re re re re do mi do.

6–7 Love Somebody
Valentine's Day, February 14

GRADE LEVEL: 3–5

OBJECTIVE: Students will label symbolic notation with syllables. Students will identify matching melodic patterns. Students will read, sing, and play a melody.

MATERIALS: Master 6–7; Bells or keyboard

PREPARATION: Make a transparency and student copies of Master 6–7.

Directions: Distribute student copies of Master 6–7. Display transparency. Sing the song using syllables rather than lyrics. Instruct students to fill in syllable names. Follow the notation as students sing the syllables. Analyze each phrase for its melodic contour. Write a letter in each box to illustrate the form of this song. Allow time for students to play the song on bells or keyboard.

ANSWER KEY: 1. A; do mi sol sol re mi fa.
2. A´; do mi sol sol fa mi re.
3. A; do mi sol sol re mi fa.
4. B; mi mi re re re re do mi do.

6–8 Lovely Rhythms
Valentine's Day, February 14

GRADE LEVEL: 1–8

OBJECTIVE: Students will write rhythm patterns from dictation.

MATERIALS: Master 6–10; one rhythm instrument (for example, triangle)

PREPARATION: Prepare six rhythm patterns of appropriate difficulty. Make student copies of Master 6–10.

DIRECTIONS: Distribute student copies of Master 6–10. Play rhythm patterns on a rhythm instrument. Allow time after each pattern for students to write the pattern they hear. To adapt this activity for any grade level, vary the difficulty of the patterns by length and by rhythmic content. Younger students may write patterns in icons, stick notation, or other nontraditional form as appropriate for their abilities.

6–9 The Minute Waltz
Frédéric Chopin, February 22

GRADE LEVEL: 4–8

OBJECTIVE: Students will analyze "The Minute Waltz."

MATERIALS: Master 6–9; recording of Frédéric Chopin's Waltz in D♭ Major

PREPARATION: Make student copies of Master 6–9.

DIRECTIONS: Distribute student copies. Clarify instructions if necessary. Play the recording as many times as necessary for students to complete all answers. Discuss answers. Relisten to correct and confirm answers.

6–10 William Tell Overture
Giacchino Rossini, February 29

GRADE LEVEL: 4–8

OBJECTIVE: Students will follow a listening map.

MATERIALS: Master 6–10; recording of Giacchino Rossini's *William Tell* Overture

PREPARATION: Make a transparency and student copies of Master 6–10.

DIRECTIONS: Display transparency. Play finale and coda sections of *William Tell* Overture. Instruct students to follow the map as you point out the musical events and sections. Distribute student copies. Replay the recording of the finale and coda. Invite students to follow their own copies, but continue to point out events on the transparency. Play the recording additional times (on subsequent class meetings) until students are able to keep their places accurately as they follow their own copies of the map. Listen to the entire overture during subsequent class periods, using other sections of the map. Note: Map sections I and III suggest musical content only and may serve as a springboard for student-generated maps.

6–11 February Melodies
Presidents' Day, Third Monday in February

GRADE LEVEL: 3–8

OBJECTIVE: Students will write melodic patterns from dictation.

MATERIALS: Master 6–11; one melody instrument (for example, piano, bellset)

PREPARATION: Prepare six melody patterns of appropriate difficulty. Make student copies of Master 6–11.

DIRECTIONS: Distribute student copies of Master 6–11. Establish tonality and play each pattern. Allow time after each pattern for students to write the pattern they hear. To adapt this activity for any grade level, vary the difficulty of the patterns by length and by melodic content. Younger students may write patterns in nontraditional form as appropriate for their abilities.

Name _____ **Date** _____

6–1   **Take Care of Your Grin**

Directions: Compose a song about your teeth. Use these bells.

| C | D | E | | G | A |

Write one letter in each box.

Take	care	of	your	grin,

Take	care	of	your	grin,

Or you'll	need	a		cup

To	put	it	in.

Sing and play your song. Sing verse two words as you play your melody.

Verse two:

Brush three times a day,
Brush three times a day.
And you'll say goodbye
To tooth decay.

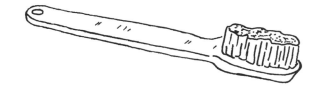

Name _____   Date _____

6–2   **Will We Have More Winter?**

1. Play and sing this song. Use these bells.

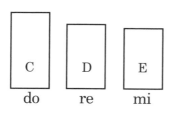

C	D	E		G	A
do	re	mi		sol	la

sol	sol	la	la	sol	mi
Can	you	see	your	shad-	ow,

sol	sol	la	la	sol	
From	your	lit	- tle	hill?	———

sol	sol	la	la	sol	mi
Will	we	have	more	win -	ter,

sol	fa	mi	re	do	
Punx-	su-	taw	-ney	Phil?	—————

2. Use your ears to arrange these bells in order from lowest to highest.

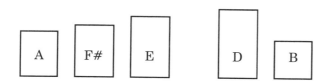

A	F#	E		D	B

3. Label the bells: do   re   mi   sol   la
4. Play and sing "Will We Have More Winter?" in a new key.

Name _____   **Date** _____

6–3   ## Invent a Musical Instrument

PLAN YOUR INSTRUMENT

Your completed plans will be due on: _____.

    1. How will you play it?   _____ by blowing into it

                                        _____ by striking it

                                        _____ by strumming it

                                        _____ other: _____

    2. Sketch your instrument here.

    3. What will you need to build it? _____

          _____   _____

          _____   _____

          _____   _____

    4. What will you name your instrument? _____

BUILD YOUR INSTRUMENT

    Your completed instrument will be due on _____.

DEMONSTRATE YOUR INSTRUMENT

    Your demonstration is scheduled for _____.

6–4   **Love to Me, Love to You**

1.
Love   to   me,   love   to   you,

Some - one   loves   you,   I   know   who.

Check   your   mail - box,   have   some   fun.

Val - en - tine,   Val - en - tine,   you   got   one.

2. Love to me, love to you,
   Someone loves you, I know who.
   Check your mailbox, tie your shoe,
   Valentine, Valentine, you got two.

3. Love to me, love to you,
   Someone loves you, I know who.
   Check your mailbox, bend your knee,
   Valentine, Valentine, you got three.

4. Love to me, love to you,
   Someone loves you, I know who.
   Check your mailbox, knock on the door,
   Valentine, Valentine, you got four.

5. Love to me, love to you,
   Someone loves you, I know who.
   Check your mailbox, start to jive,
   Valentine, Valentine, you got five.

6. Love to me, love to you,
   Someone loves you, I know who.
   Check your mailbox, play some tricks,
   Valentine, Valentine, you got six.

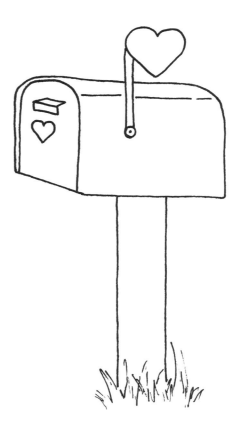

Name _____   Date _____

Love to Me, Love to You

Directions: Duplicate hearts on heavy paper or tagboard. Color and cut out. Use with Master 6–4.

Name _____   **Date** _____

6–6   **Love Somebody**

Directions: Fill in the missing syllable names. Draw one shape in each box to show the form of this song. Sing and play the song.

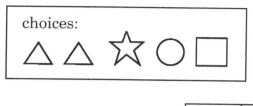

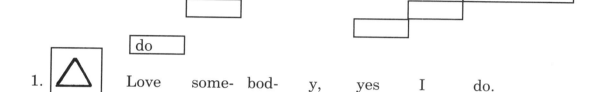

1. Love   some- bod-   y,   yes   I   do.

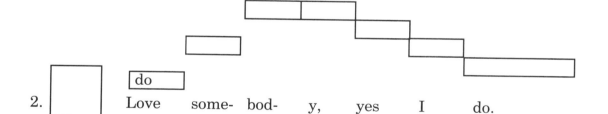

2. Love   some- bod-   y,   yes   I   do.

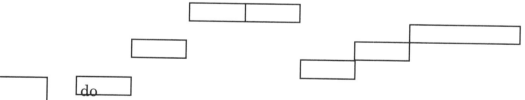

3. Love   some- bod-   y,   yes   I   do.

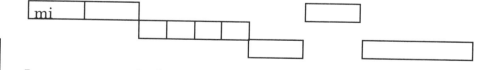

4. Love   some- bod-y   but I   won't   tell   who.

© 1992 by Loretta Mitchell

Name _____   **Date** _____

6–7   **Love Somebody**

Directions: Fill in the missing syllable names. Write a letter in each box to show the form of this song. Sing and play the song.

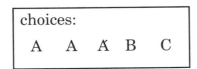

1.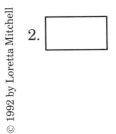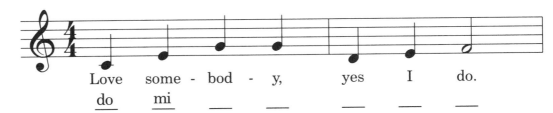

Love   some - bod - y,   yes   I   do.
<u>do</u>   <u>mi</u>   ___   ___   ___   ___   ___

2.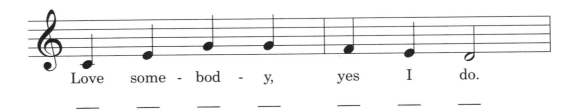

Love   some - bod - y,   yes   I   do.
___   ___   ___   ___   ___   ___   ___

3.

Love   some - bod - y,   yes   I   do.
___   ___   ___   ___   ___   ___   ___

4.

Love   some - bod - y   but   I   won't   tell   who.
___   ___   ___   ___   ___   ___   ___   ___

choices:

A   A   A´   B   C

© 1992 by Loretta Mitchell

 **6–8** Lovely Rhythms

1.

2.

3.

4.

5.

6.

Name _____   Date _____

6–9   **The Minute Waltz**

by Frédéric Chopin

Frédéric Chopin titled this music Waltz in D♭ Major when he composed it. "The Minute Waltz" is its nickname.

Directions: Listen to a recording of "The Minute Waltz." Answer the following questions.

1. Name the instrument you hear playing.

   _____

2. How does this music move? Circle your answer.

   In twos   In threes   In fours

3. Which picture best describes the form of this music? Circle your answer.

4. Time the music as you listen.

   Write the starting time here: _____

   Write the ending time here: _____

   How long did the composition last? _____

5. Look up the word *minute* in the dictionary.

   Find a definition for the word when it is pronounced "mĭn´ŭt."

   Write that definition here: _____

   Find a definition for the word when it is pronounced "mī nūt´."

   Write that definition here: _____

6. Which definition of *minute* is best for this waltz?

   _____

   Why? _____

6–10 **William Tell Overture**

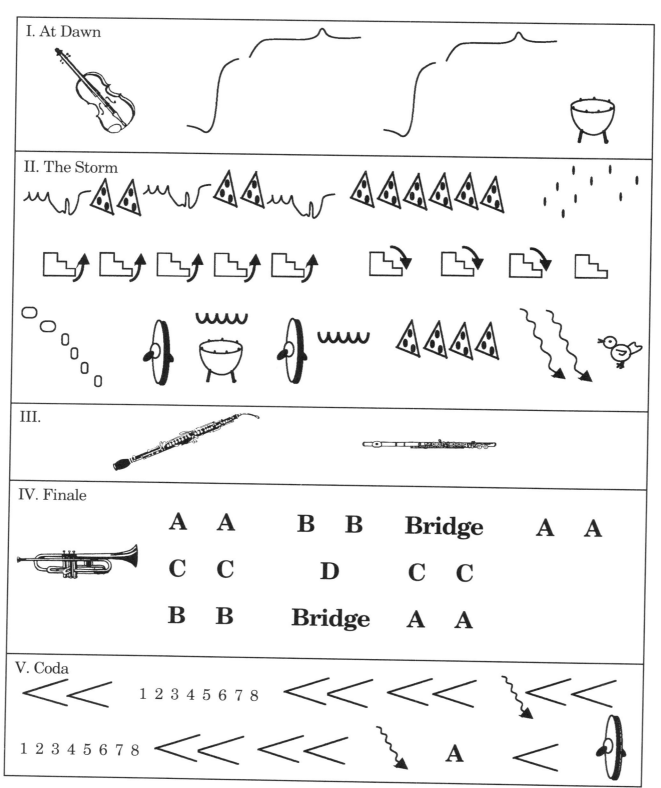

I. At Dawn

II. The Storm

III.

IV. Finale

A	A	B	B	Bridge	A	A
C	C	D	C	C
B	B	Bridge	A	A

V. Coda

1 2 3 4 5 6 7 8

1 2 3 4 5 6 7 8

A

Name _____ **Date** _____

6–11

February Melodies

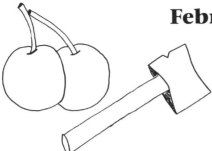 

1.

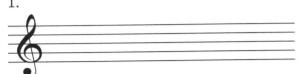

2.

3.

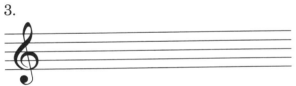

4.

5.

6.

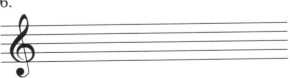

MARCH
TEACHER'S GUIDE

7-1 Celebrate Music Education
Music in Our Schools Month

GRADE LEVEL: 4-8

OBJECTIVE: Students will discuss and write about the importance of music in their lives.

MATERIALS: Master 7-1

PREPARATION: Make student copies of Master 7-1.

DIRECTIONS: Initiate a discussion about the importance of music in our lives. You may wish to start with questions such as:

What would your life be like without music?

What will music be like in 10 years? 50 years? 200 years?

Why do people spend their money on sound equipment, concerts, and recordings?

Why do some musicians become famous and have fan clubs?

Instruct students to write about their own feelings, completing the statement on Master 7-1. Cut around the piano outlines, and display your students' work in the school and the community.

7-2 Peanuts Peanuts Peanuts
National Peanut Month

GRADE LEVEL: 4-6

OBJECTIVE: Students will perform a rhythmic chant with instrumental accompaniment and an ostinato.

MATERIALS: Master 7-2; suspended cymbal and brush

PREPARATION: Make student copies of Master 7-2.

DIRECTIONS: Help students read the rhythms and learn the chant. Select soloists and small groups. Add one or both ostinati. Add the cymbal accompaniment. Encourage students' creative suggestions for other accompaniment possibilities. Add an introduction and a coda.

7–3 **The Swing Era**
Glenn Miller, March 1

GRADE LEVEL: 4–8

OBJECTIVE: Students will identify music from the Swing Era.

MATERIALS: Master 7–3; recordings of Swing Era hits

PREPARATION: Make student copies of Master 7–3.

DIRECTIONS: Distribute student copies. Play one recording. Help students list the title, the name of the band, and one musical characteristic (for example, improvised trombone solo). Continue with other Swing Era recordings. To complete the last column on the grid, instruct students to take the page home and to find one adult (neighbor, friend, or relative) who recognizes each title and agrees to sign the page. OPTIONAL: Offer an award or incentive for the person who secures the most signatures.

7–4 **O'er the Ramparts**
National Anthem Day, March 3

GRADE LEVEL: 4–8

OBJECTIVE: Students will dramatize events that led to the writing of our national anthem.

MATERIALS: Master 7–4; piano accompaniment for "The Star-Spangled Banner" (optional)

PREPARATION: Make student copies of Master 7–4.

DIRECTIONS: Distribute student copies. Assign parts. Read through the play. Allow students who do not have speaking parts to read the words to the national anthem on the last page of Master 7–4. Sing the national anthem at the end of the play. OPTIONAL: Add costumes, scenery, and props and perform the play.

7–5 **A Star-Spangled Melody**
National Anthem Day, March 3

GRADE LEVEL: 3–6

OBJECTIVE: Students will sequence melodic icons from "The Star-Spangled Banner."

MATERIALS: Master 7–5; scissors for each student

PREPARATION: Adjust the level of difficulty of this exercise by numbering one or more of the melody blocks before you duplicate the master. Make student copies of Master 7–5. Be sure that students are familiar with the melody of the song.

7–5, A Star–Spangled Melody, continued

DIRECTIONS: Decide whether students will work individually or in small groups. Lead the class in singing "The Star-Spangled Banner." Draw the melodic contour in the air as you sing. Instruct students to cut apart the melody blocks and sequence them. Give clues to simplify the process if necessary (for example, sing a phrase on syllables or scale degrees and ask students to find the matching block). Encourage students to sing the song aloud as they work. When students have correctly sequenced all eight blocks, sing the song again, following the melodic icons.

7–6 Hello, How Are You?
Anniversary of the Telephone, March 10

GRADE LEVEL: 2–4

OBJECTIVE: Students will improvise musical conversation.

MATERIALS: Master 7–6

PREPARATION: Make student copies of Master 7–6.

DIRECTIONS: Distribute student copies. Instruct students to choose partners and follow directions on their copies. Invite volunteers to perform their improvised conversation for the class.

7–7 Johnny Appleseed
Johnny Appleseed Day, March 11

GRADE LEVEL: 1–3

OBJECTIVE: Students will perform and respond to verse-refrain form.

MATERIALS: Master 7–7

PREPARATION: Make one copy of Master 7–7.

DIRECTIONS: Teach this song by rote. Speak the verses. Sing the refrain. Encourage student suggestions for movement or body percussion to add to the verses and refrain (for example, clap the beat on the verses or draw the melodic contour in the air on the refrain).

7–8 Paddy Works on the Railway
St. Patrick's Day, March 17

GRADE LEVEL: 3–5

OBJECTIVE: Students will create new verses for a folk song.

MATERIALS: Master 7–8; recording of "Paddy Works on the Railway" (optional)

PREPARATION: Make student copies of Master 7–8.

DIRECTIONS: Help students learn to sing the song. Analyze the repetitive pattern and rhyme scheme of the lyrics. Create verse two as a class. Challenge students to create verses three and four individually. Invite volunteers to share their verses with the class. OPTIONAL: Play a recording of this song to allow students to compare their verses to the recorded version.

7–9   Little Fugue in G Minor
J.S. Bach, March 21

GRADE LEVEL: 4–8

OBJECTIVE: Students will follow a map of a fugue.

MATERIALS: Master 7–9; recording of J. S. Bach's Little Fugue in G Minor

PREPARATION: Make a transparency and student copies of Master 7–9.

DIRECTIONS: Introduce or review the structure of a fugue. Display transparency. Sing or play the fugue subject. Play the recording in segments, allowing students to identify subject occurrences in each section. Finally, play the entire recording and allow students to follow the map without assistance. On subsequent hearings, invite students' attention to the countersubject or to episodes.

7–10, 7–11   Happy Birthday, Dear Sebastian
J. S. Bach, March 21

GRADE LEVEL: 4–8

OBJECTIVE: Students will celebrate J. S. Bach's birthday.

MATERIALS: Masters 7–10, 7–11; Bach recordings; art supplies; party supplies; refreshments

PREPARATION: Study the life and works of J. S. Bach. Make a transparency and student copies of Master 7–11.

DIRECTIONS: Display transparency. Discuss plans for your party. Divide the class into small groups. Assign one or more tasks to each group. Help the class sequence the tasks and establish deadlines for each. Distribute copies of Master 7–11. Help each group follow instructions on Master 7–11. When plans are completed, implement the plans and have a great celebration!

7–12 Surprise Symphony
Franz Joseph Haydn, March 31

GRADE LEVEL: 4–6

OBJECTIVE: Students will describe theme and variations form.

MATERIALS: Master 7–12; recording of Franz Joseph Haydn's Symphony No. 94 in G Major, second movement: Andante; Master 5–11 (optional)

PREPARATION: Make student copies of Master 7–12.

DIRECTIONS: Distribute student copies of Master 7–12. Discuss the concept of "Theme and Variations" in a musical context. OPTIONAL: Refer to Master 5–11 to reinforce theme and variations concepts. Play the recording and call out numbers to identify each variation as it occurs. Clarify student instructions if necessary. Allow students several opportunities to hear the recording if necessary.

ANSWER KEY:
a. Variation 3   b. Variation 1   c. Variation 4
d. Theme   e. Coda   f. Variation 2

7–13 Lions and Lambs

GRADE LEVEL: 3–5

OBJECTIVE: Students will identify and apply music reading symbols.

MATERIALS: Master 7–13; music texts

PREPARATION: Make student copies of Master 7–13.

DIRECTIONS: Distribute student copies. Instruct students to draw lines to match music symbols with their correct definitions. Distribute music texts. Invite students to find one occurrence of each music symbol in their books. Sing the selected songs.

7–14 Let's Go Fly a Kite

GRADE LEVEL: 3–6

OBJECTIVE: Students will create movement to describe verse-refrain form.

MATERIALS: Master 7–14; recording of "Let's Go Fly a Kite" from *Mary Poppins*

PREPARATION: Make a transparency of Master 7–14. Make one copy of Master 7–14 for each group.

DIRECTIONS: Play the recording. Display transparency. Help class identify and follow the verse-refrain form. Divide class members into groups of three or four members. Instruct groups to create movement as follows: (1) For each verse, dramatize or express in another way the melodic, rhythmic, or lyric content, (2) For the refrain, create one movement sequence that is to be duplicated each time the refrain occurs. Groups should appoint a person who will record the plan on Master 7–14. Give groups time to rehearse and perform their movement plans.

7–15 Windy Days of March

GRADE LEVEL: 3–5

OBJECTIVE: Students will plan and perform a sound piece.

MATERIALS: Master 7–15; sound sources (for example, classroom instruments)

PREPARATION: Make a transparency of Master 7–15.

DIRECTIONS: Display transparency. Encourage student suggestions of March sounds and ideas for re-creating them in the classroom. For variety, assign sounds to soloists, small groups, and the full class. Follow instructions on Master 7–15. After your performance, select another conductor, and perform again.

Name _____ Date _____

Music is Important to Me

7–2   **Peanuts Peanuts Peanuts**

1. *all*   Peanuts roasted in the shell,

   all   Peanut vendors buy and sell.

2. *solo 1*   Roasted dry and roasted light,
   all   Munch on peanuts morn' 'til night.

3. *solo 2*   Light salt,
   solo 3   no salt,
   solo 4   take your pick,
   all   Eat 'em slow or eat 'em quick.

4. *girl solo 5*   Peanut butter,
   girl solo 6   Peanut oil,
   all girls   Peanut choc'late sundae royal.

5. *boy solo 7*   Peanut icing,
   boy solo 8   Peanut cake,
   all boys   Peanut recipes to bake.

6. *small group 1*   Peanut brittle,
   small group 2   Peanut crunch,
   all   Peanut cookies after lunch.

7. *small group 3*   Eat a peanut just for fun,
   solo 9   Not a soul can eat just one.

8. *all*   Shout from rooftops, sing and yell,
   all   That's our tale in a peanut shell.

Ostinato 1: Peanuts roasted in the shell

Ostinato 2: Um   peanuts

Cymbal and brush:

Name _____   Date _____

7–3   **The Swing Era**

	TITLE	PERFORMER/ BAND	ONE MUSICAL CHARACTERISTIC	SIGNATURE OF AN ADULT
1.				
2.				
3.				
4.				
5.				
6.				

7–4   **O'er the Ramparts**

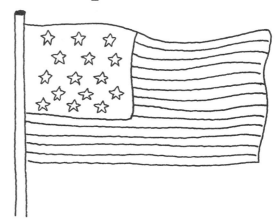

Characters: Narrator 1
              Narrator 2
              Narrator 3
              Francis Scott Key
              Colonel John Skinner
              Dr. William Beane
              British Admiral

Narrator 1: It was the year 1814. The British and Americans were back at war, the War of 1812.

Narrator 2: A British Navy ship, anchored off Fort McHenry, was holding an elderly American prisoner, Dr. William Beane.

Narrator 3: Francis Scott Key, a young American attorney, and Colonel John Skinner were given American authorization to take a small sailing vessel out to the British ship to try to negotiate the release of Dr. Beane.

Francis Scott Key: Permission to come aboard, Sir.

British Admiral: Permission granted.

Francis Scott Key: We have come to discuss the release of American prisoner, Dr. William Beane. In return, we are willing to release British prisoners.

British Admiral: Do you have any paperwork with you?

Colonel Skinner: Yes, sir, we have this letter from the American government.

British Admiral: Well, I will have to study this proposal.

Francis Scott Key: As you wish, sir. We will wait.

Narrator 1: So Francis Scott Key and Colonel Skinner waited aboard the British ship.

Narrator 2: Soon, the British agreed to let Dr. Beane leave in the small boat with Key and Skinner.

Narrator 3: The Americans were just ready to board their small boat when the admiral stopped them abruptly.

British Admiral: Stop! You cannot leave!

7–4, O'er the Ramparts, continued

Francis Scott Key: But why, sir? With all respect, you did agree to the release of this prisoner.

British Admiral: You have been aboard this vessel too long. You may have heard our plans to attack Fort McHenry tonight. If we allow you to go back to the fort tonight, you might disclose our plans.

Colonel Skinner: But, sir, we haven't heard a thing!

British Admiral: Nevertheless, we must take every precaution to keep our attack a surprise. You will stay on board tonight.

Colonel Skinner: As you wish, Admiral.

Narrator 1:   So the Americans resigned themselves to a night on the British vessel.

Narrator 2:   The battle began. As darkness came, they could no longer see the fort. How they wanted to know what was happening on shore!

Narrator 3:   Their only clue was a flagpole, bearing the stars and stripes. They riveted their eyes upon it, knowing that, as long as it waved, the Americans were winning.

Dr. Beane: Oh, Francis, it is getting harder to see. How ever will we know who is winning?

Francis Scott Key: Watch the flag, gentlemen. We will hope and pray that the flag of the United States continues to wave over the fort.

Narrator 1:   With every flash of bursting bombs, they peered through the darkness to see if the flag was still waving.

Colonel Skinner: With all this smoke, I cannot make out whose flag is on the flagpole! Francis, can you see?

Francis Scott Key: No, I cannot see. Oh, yes, there it is! Our flag is still waving!

Narrator 2:   And so it continued, throughout the night. The Americans watched fearfully for their flag through the smoke-filled skies. Occasionally the burst of bombs lighted the sky enough to illuminate the flagpole.

Narrator 3:   When dawn came, the men were exhausted from their nightlong vigil. They waited eagerly for enough sunlight to see the flagpole.

Dr. Beane: Can you see it, gentlemen? Is it there?

7–4, O'er the Ramparts, continued

Francis Scott Key:	I cannot see anything! There's too much smoke!
Colonel Skinner:	It's getting lighter now. Perhaps we will see it soon.
Francis Scott Key:	Dr. Beane! Colonel! I see it! Our flag is still there! Quick! I need some paper. I must write down my thoughts!
Colonel Skinner:	Don't you have an envelope in your coat pocket?
Francis Scott Key:	Yes, yes! I must write this down before I forget it!
Francis Scott Key:	*(writing as he speaks)*

O say can you see by the dawn's early light
What so proudly we hailed at the twilight's last gleaming,
Whose broad stripes and bright stars, through the perilous fight,
O'er the ramparts we watched were so gallantly streaming?
And the rockets' red glare, the bombs bursting in air,
Gave proof through the night that our flag was still there.
O say does that star-spangled banner yet wave
O'er the land of the free and the home of the brave?

Narrator 1:	Francis wrote verses two and three as they sailed back to shore. He revised the poem later that evening in his hotel room. The poem was printed and distributed on handbills the next day.
Narrator 2:	Later it was sung to a popular tune of the times.
Narrator 3:	In 1931, Congress declared "The Star-Spangled Banner" as our official U.S. National Anthem.
Narrator 1:	Please stand and join us as we sing our national anthem.

[Cast and audience sing "The Star-Spangled Banner."]

THE END

Date _____

7-5

A Star-Spangled Melody

Directions: Sing "The Star-Spangled Banner." Draw the melody in the air as you sing. Cut these blocks apart. Arrange them in the correct order to create the melody of our national anthem. When you have them in the correct order, sing "The Star-Spangled Banner" again. Follow your melody blocks as you sing.

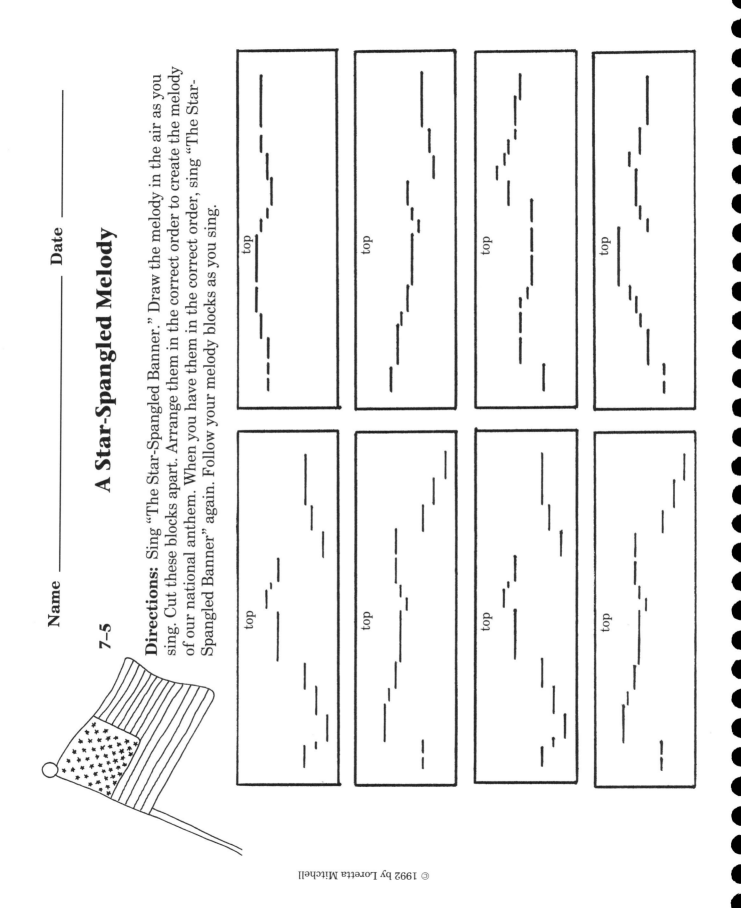

Name _____   **Date** _____

7–6   **Hello, How Are You?**

1. Choose a partner. One partner will be A. The other partner will be B. Follow the plan below and make up a conversation using your normal speaking voice.

    A: RRRRRINGGGGG!

    B: Hello.

    A: Hello, _____ , this is _____ .

    B: Oh, hi, _____ , I'm glad you called.

    A: I called to ask you _____ .

    B: _____ .

    A: _____ .

    (Continue the conversation as long as you wish.)

    B: _____ .

    A: Well, thank you, _____ . Goodbye.

    B: Goodbye, _____ .

2. Repeat your conversation, using your singing voices. YOU MUST SING EVERY WORD!

7–7   **Johnny Appleseed**

1. Jonathan Chapman was his name.
   Johnny Appleseed he became.

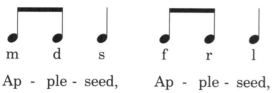

m   d   s   f   r   l

Ap - ple - seed,   Ap - ple - seed,

s   f   m   r   m   d   d

Call   on John - ny Ap - ple - seed.

2. Johnny traveled long ago
   Near the River O - HI - O.

3. Wore no shoes, or so it's said.
   A pot of tin upon his head.

Make up verses four and five.

4. _____

   _____

   _____

5. _____

   _____

   _____

7–8   ## Paddy Works on the Railway

In eigh-teen hun-dred and for-ty-one, I put me cor-du-roy brit-ches on.

I put me cor-du-roy brit-ches on, to work up-on the rail - way.

Refrain

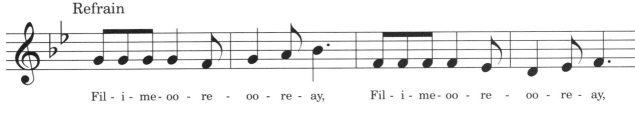

Fil - i - me-oo - re - oo - re - ay,   Fil - i - me-oo - re - oo - re - ay,

Fil - i - me-oo - re - oo - re - ay, to work up-on the rail - way.

Create new words for verses two through four:

2. In eighteen hundred and forty–two,
   I _____
   I _____
   To work upon the railway.

3. In eighteen hundred and forty-three,
   I _____
   I _____
   To work upon the railway.

4. In eighteen hundred and forty-four,
   I _____
   I _____
   To work upon the railway.

Name _____   **Date** _____

7–9   # Little Fugue in G Minor

by J. S. Bach

Directions: Sing or play the beginning of Bach's fugue SUBJECT:

This fugue has four voices: soprano, alto, tenor, and bass. In the EXPOSITION, each voice states the subject.

s

a

t

b

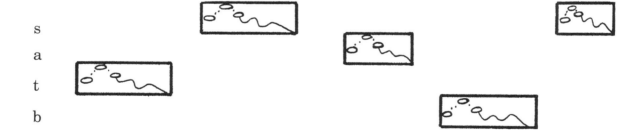

In the DEVELOPMENT, the subject is stated five or more times.

s

a

t

b

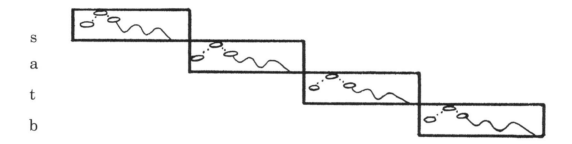

In the RECAPITULATION, all voices join together to state the subject one final time.

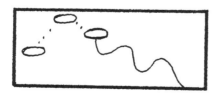

Name _____   Date _____

7–10   **Happy Birthday, Dear Sebastian**

Directions: Plan a birthday party for Johann Sebastian Bach. Celebrate his life and his musical masterpieces. Start by planning your party.

1. When will you have the party?_____
2. Where will you hold the party?_____
3. Divide the tasks. Assign one task to each group.

GROUP 1 TASK: Make your guest list. Deadline:_____

Guest List
_____   _____   _____
_____   _____   _____
_____   _____   _____
_____   _____   _____
_____   _____   _____
_____   _____   _____

GROUP 2 TASK: Design your invitation. Deadline:_____

GROUP 3 TASK: Mail or deliver the invitations. Deadline:_____

GROUP 4 TASK: Plan the entertainment. Deadline:_____
How will you entertain the guests? How could you use Bach's music at your party?

GROUP 5 TASK: Plan and serve refreshments. Deadline:_____

GROUP 6 TASK: Clean-up. Deadline:_____

Name _____   Date _____

7–11   # Happy Birthday, Dear Sebastian

GROUP NUMBER _____ Members _____ _____ _____ _____

YOUR TASK _____ **DEADLINE** _____

PLAN
What is your plan to accomplish your task?

Step 1 _____   Step 2 _____

Step 3 _____   Step 4 _____

TIME LINE
What is your deadline? _____

How will you meet your deadline? _____

_____

MATERIALS AND EQUIPMENT

What will you need? _____ _____ _____ _____

_____ _____ _____ _____

GETTING THE JOB DONE
How will you divide up the work so that each group member has a job?
When does each job have to be completed?

name	job	deadline
name	job	deadline
name	job	deadline
name	job	deadline

Name _____ **Date** _____

7–12 # Surprise Symphony
by Franz Joseph Haydn

Directions: This is a theme composed by Haydn. Sing or play this theme.

Listen to the second movement of Haydn's Surprise Symphony. You will hear the theme more than once. As you listen, find a description of each variation to match what you are hearing. Label each box with the correct variation number.

Choices:	Theme	Variation 2	Variation 4
	Variation 1	Variation 3	Coda

a.

countermelody

b.

countermelody

c.

Brasses and woodwinds | Full orchestra **ff**

d.

staccato

e.

p

f.

minor **f/p**

Name _____ **Date** _____

7–13   **Lions and Lambs**

Directions: Match the music symbols on the left with the definitions on the right. Find each symbol in your music book. Write the page number in each box. Sing the songs and use each music symbol correctly.

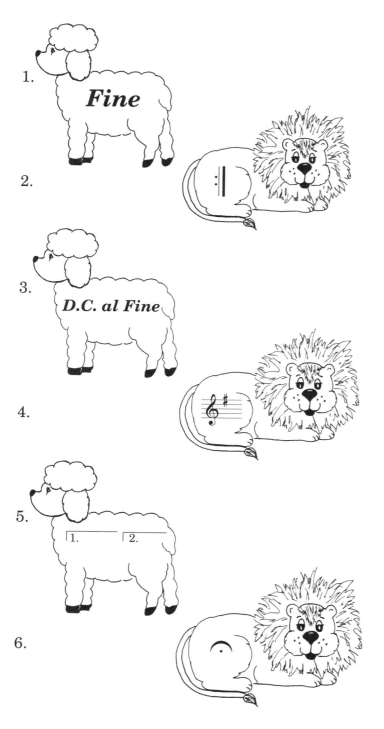

1. *Fine*

2.

3. *D.C. al Fine*

4.

5.

6.

Stop, the end.

page ____

Go back to the beginning of the song. End at Fine.

page ____

Repeat sign. Sing this part again.

page ____

Fermata. Hold this note longer.

page ____

First and second endings.

page ____

Key signature of one sharp.

page ____

Name _____   Date _____

7–14   **Let's Go Fly a Kite**
                    Words and Music by Richard M. Sherman and Robert B. Shermam

Section	Write or sketch your movement plan here:
Introduction	
Verse One	
Refrain	
Verse Two	
Refrain	Same as the first refrain

7–15   # Windy Days of March

Directions: Find ways to make these March sounds. Use body percussion, instruments, or sound sources you find in the classroom. Add more sounds to the map. Select a conductor and perform.

laundry flapping on the
clothesline

tree branches swaying

wind whistling

window shutters clattering

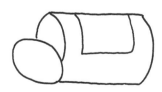

a tin can clanging
across the street

157

APRIL
TEACHER'S GUIDE

8–1, 8–2 April Fool
April Fool's Day, April 1

GRADE LEVEL: 1–3

OBJECTIVE: Students will create verses for a song.

MATERIALS: Masters 8–1, 8–2

PREPARATION: Make a copy of Master 8–1. Enlarge Master 8–2. Color the picture cards and cut apart.

DIRECTIONS: Teach the song by rote. Use picture cards to help teach additional verses. Encourage students to create additional verses. Invite students to illustrate their suggestions. Add their drawings to the card collection.

EXTENSION: Make your song cumulative. In each verse, repeat a portion of the preceding verse(s).

2. There's a horse in your bathtub,
   fish in your coffee, April Fool,

5. There's a skunk in your bedroom,
   bee in your pocket,
   bear in your schoolbus,
   horse in your bathtub,
   fish in your coffee . . .

8–3 They Call It Barbershop
Barbershop Quartet Day, April 11

GRADE LEVEL: 4–8

OBJECTIVE: Students will create four-part harmony.

MATERIALS: Master 8–3

PREPARATION: Make a transparency and student copies of Master 8–3.

DIRECTIONS: Divide the class into four groups. Help students play and sing their parts. Layer the four parts, starting with the lead, adding one more part at a time until you have all four performing together.

EXTENSION: (1) Play a recording of a barbershop quartet. If you have difficulty finding recorded examples, contact your local chapter of the Society for the

Preservation and Encouragement of Barbershop Quartets Singing in America (SPEBSQSA). (2) Play a videotape of the movie *The Music Man*. (3) Invite a local barbershop quartet to perform for your class. (4) Arrange for your class to attend a rehearsal or concert of a local barbershop group.

8–4 I Love to Read
National Library Week

GRADE LEVEL: 2–3

OBJECTIVE: Students will compose a pentatonic song.

MATERIALS: Master 8–4; bellsets; mallets; pencils

PREPARATION: Make a copy of Master 8–4.

DIRECTIONS: Decide whether students will work individually or in small groups. Clarify instructions if necessary. Allow time for students to compose. Encourage students to perform their compositions for the class. Accompany student compositions with the following:

8–5 It's Time to Turn to Spring

GRADE LEVEL: K–1

OBJECTIVE: Students will perform a finger play.

MATERIALS: Master 8–5

PREPARATION: Make one copy of Master 8–5.

DIRECTIONS: Teach the finger play by rote. Teach the actions with the words.

8–6 What Do We Plant When We Plant the Tree?
Arbor Day

GRADE LEVEL: 5–8

OBJECTIVE: Students will perform a choral reading with instrumental

8–6, *What Do We Plant When We Plant the Tree?*, continued

accompaniment.

MATERIALS: Master 8–6; rhythm instruments

PREPARATION: Make a transparency of Master 8–6.

DIRECTIONS: Display transparency. Invite students to read through the poem together. Use a dictionary to define any unfamiliar words. Assign solos and small group parts. Rehearse the poem. Add instruments as suggested on Master 8–6. Perform the poem with accompaniment. Encourage student suggestions for expression and other accompaniment ideas. Make changes and perform again.

8–7, 8–8 Peter and the Wolf
Sergei Prokofiev, April 23

GRADE LEVEL: K–3

OBJECTIVE: Students will identify themes and instruments in a famous composition.

MATERIALS: Masters 8–7, 8–8; envelopes, two per student; recording of Sergei Prokofiev's *Peter and the Wolf*

PREPARATION: Make student copies of Masters 8–7 and 8–8. Cut apart student cards (Master 8–8). Place each set of character cards in an envelope. Place each set of instrument cards in an envelope.

DIRECTIONS: Tell the story of Peter and the Wolf. Distribute one background (Master 8–7) and one set of character cards to each student. Play the recording. Instruct students to listen carefully and show what they hear by placing each character card into center stage position. During a subsequent lesson, use instrument cards in the same way.

8–9, 8–10 Easter Egg Hunt

GRADE LEVEL: 1–6

OBJECTIVE: Students will write melodic patterns from dictation.

MATERIALS: Masters 8–9, 8–10; one melody instrument (for example, piano, bellset)

PREPARATION: Prepare six melody patterns of appropriate difficulty. Make student copies of Master 8–9 or 8–10.

DIRECTIONS: Distribute student copies. Establish tonality and play each pattern. Allow time after each pattern for students to write the pattern they hear. To adapt this activity for any grade level, vary the difficulty of the patterns by length and by melodic content. Use Master 8–10 for younger students; they may write patterns in icons without using a traditional five-line staff.

8–11 Welcome Springtime

GRADE LEVEL: 1–2

OBJECTIVE: Students will sequence rhythm patterns.

MATERIALS: Master 8–11

PREPARATION: Make student copies of Master 8–11.

DIRECTIONS: Distribute student copies. Instruct students to cut out their rhythm cards. Dictate simple rhythm patterns (see sample patterns). Students will arrange their cards to describe the patterns they hear.
Sample patterns:

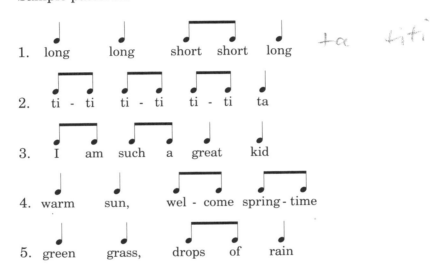

1. long   long   short short   long   ta   titi

2. ti - ti   ti - ti   ti - ti   ta

3. I   am such   a   great   kid

4. warm   sun,   wel - come   spring - time

5. green   grass,   drops   of   rain

8–12 It's Raining

GRADE LEVEL: 2–4

OBJECTIVE: Students will add harmony to a familiar song.

MATERIALS: Master 8–12; bellset or other melody instrument (optional)

PREPARATION: Make a transparency of Master 8–12.

DIRECTIONS: Teach or review the song. Display transparency. Help students read, play, or sing one of the harmony parts. Select a small group to perform the harmony. Combine the melody and the harmony.

Name _____ Date _____

8-1   **April Fool**

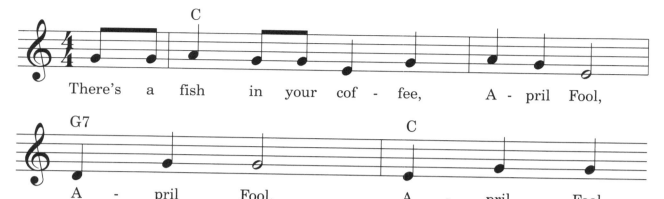

There's a fish in your cof - fee, A - pril Fool,

A - pril Fool, A - pril Fool,

There's a fish in your cof - fee, A - pril Fool,

A - pril, A - pril Fool.

2. There's a horse in your bathtub, April Fool,
   April Fool, April Fool.
   There's a horse in your bathtub, April Fool,
   April Fool, April Fool.

3. There's a bear in your schoolbus, . . .

4. There's a bee in your pocket, . . .

5. There's a skunk in your bedroom, . . .

Name _____   Date _____

April Fool

1.

2.

3.

4.

5.

Name _____ Date _____

8-3   **They Call It Barbershop**

Directions: Divide your class into four groups.
Select a player for each group. Learn to play
and sing your line. Put all four parts together
to create barbershop harmony.

Part 1: Tenor

Twin-kle, twin-kle,   lit-tle star,   how I won-der what you are, oh,   what you are!

Part 2: Lead

Twin-kle, twin-kle,   lit-tle star,   how I won-der what you are, oh,   what you are!

Part 3: Baritone

Twin-kle, twin-kle,   lit-tle star, how I won-der what you are, oh,   what you are!

Part 4: Bass

Twin-kle, twin-kle,   lit-tle star, how I won-der what you are, oh,   what you are!

Name _____ **Date** _____

8-4   **I Love to Read**

Directions: Compose a song about reading. Use these bells. Write one letter in each box.

C	D	E	G	A
do	re	mi	sol	la

Curled   up   snug   in   my   fa-   v'rite   chair,

I   can   trav-   el   an-   y -   where.

Give   me   a   book,   that's   all   I   need,

Give me   two   or   three,   I   love   to   read.

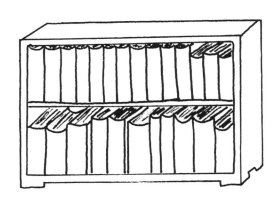

Name _____ **Date** _____

8-5 ## It's Time to Turn to Spring

Flap wings.	
Make bunny ears.	
Rub arms.	
Both hands "grow" up.	

Arms circled around face.	
Sweep arms down.	
Clap hands four times.	
Both hands "grow" up.	

Chicks and ducks, and a baby bird,

Funny little bunny rabbits, haven't you heard?

Old Man Winter, here's the word,

It's time to turn to spring.

Shine, Mr. Sun and melt the snow,

Warm the ground so the grass will grow.

Children want to play, you know,

It's time to turn to spring.

Name _____   Date _____

8-6 What Do We Plant When We Plant the Tree?

by Henry Abbey

INSTRUMENT

solo 1	none
group 1	tone block
group 2	
group 3	
solo 2	suspended cymbal
all	tone block

What do we plant when we plant the tree?

We plant the ship which will cross the sea.

We plant the mast to carry the sails,

We plant the planks to withstand the gales.

The keel, the keelson, and beam and knee,

We plant the ship when we plant the tree.

solo 1	none
group 1	tone block
group 2	
group 3	
solo 3	suspended cymbal
all	tone block

What do we plant when we plant the tree?

We plant the houses for you and me.

We plant the rafters, the shingles, the floors,

We plant the studding, the lath, the doors,

The beams and siding, all parts that be,

We plant the house when we plant the tree.

solo 1	none
group 1	tone block
group 2	
group 3	
solo 4	suspended cymbal
all	tone block

What do we plant when we plant the tree?

A thousand things that we daily see,

We plant the spire that out-towers the crag.

We plant the staff for our country's flag.

We plant the shade from the hot sun free;

We plant all these when we plant the tree.

Name _____   Date _____

8-7

Peter and the Wolf
by Sergei Prokofiev

Name _____

Date _____

8-8

Peter and the Wolf
by Sergei Prokofiev

CHARACTER CARDS

Peter	bird	duck
Grandfather	cat	wolf
		hunters

8-8, *Peter and the Wolf, continued*

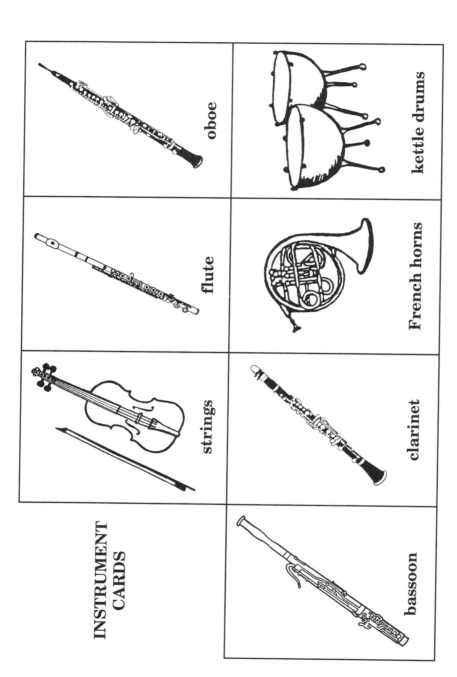

INSTRUMENT CARDS

oboe

flute

strings

clarinet

French horns

kettle drums

bassoon

Name _____ Date _____

8-9   **Easter Egg Hunt**

8-10   **Easter Egg Hunt**

Name _____   Date _____

8-11   **Welcome Springtime**

Name _____   Date _____

8-12   **It's Raining**

Sing this song.

It's rain - ing, it's pour - ing, the

Old man is snor - ing. He

Went to bed and he bumped his head and he

Could - n't get up in the morn - ing.

Learn to sing one of these harmony parts. Add it to the song.

Pit - ter, pat - ter, rain is fall - ing.

Rain - drops fall - ing down.

175

MAY
TEACHER'S GUIDE

9–1 May Baskets
May Day, May 1

GRADE LEVEL: 2–6

OBJECTIVE: Students will write melodic patterns from dictation.

MATERIALS: Master 9–1; one melody instrument (for example, piano or bellset)

PREPARATION: Prepare six melody patterns of appropriate difficulty. Make student copies of Master 9–1.

DIRECTIONS: Distribute student copies. Establish tonality and play each pattern. Allow time after each pattern for students to write the pattern they hear. To adapt this activity for any grade level, vary the difficulty of the patterns by length and by melodic content.

9–2 A Tisket, A Tasket
May Day, May 1

GRADE LEVEL: 2–4

OBJECTIVE: Students will read icons, play a melody, and transfer iconic notation to symbolic notation.

MATERIALS: Master 9–2; bellsets; mallets; pencils

PREPARATION: Make a transparency and student copies of Master 9–2.

DIRECTIONS: Determine whether students will work individually or in small groups. Distribute student copies. Clarify instructions if necessary. Allow ample time for students to read the icons and play the song. Help students complete the symbolic notation at the bottom of the page.

9–3 Long-Eared Personages
Be Kind to Animals Week

GRADE LEVEL: 1–3

OBJECTIVE: Students will describe melodic movement and follow a listening map.

MATERIALS: Master 9–3; recording of Camille Saint-Saëns's *Carnival of the Animals*

PREPARATION: Make a transparency and student copies of Master 9–3.

DIRECTIONS: Play the recording of "Long-Eared Personages." Discuss the distinctive melodic figure with the class. Invite students to create movement to describe the melodic figure. Display transparency. Distribute copies of Master 9–3. Help students follow the melodic map.

9–4 Royal March of the Lion
Be Kind to Animals Week

GRADE LEVEL: 1–3

OBJECTIVE: Students will describe rhythmic and melodic movement and follow a listening map.

MATERIALS: Master 9–4; recording of Camille Saint-Saëns's *Carnival of the Animals*

PREPARATION: Make student copies of Master 9–4.

DIRECTIONS: Play the recording of "Introduction" and "Royal March of the Lion." Help students identify the "Introduction" as "get ready music," and use it as preparatory to the "Royal March." Once the march begins, help students tap the beat in their palms as they listen. For each lion's "roar," invite students to raise their hands high in the air. Distribute copies of Master 9–4. Help students touch the lion's paws as they hear the beat and trace the "roar" icon for each lion's roar. Play the recording several times.

9–5 Fossils
Be Kind to Animals Week

GRADE LEVEL: 1–3

OBJECTIVE: Students will follow a listening map.

MATERIALS: Master 9–5; recording of Camille Saint-Saëns's *Carnival of the Animals*

PREPARATION: Make a transparency and student copies of Master 9–5.

DIRECTIONS: Play the recording of "Fossils." Invite students to stand on the "A" sections and sit on the contrasting sections. Display transparency. Distribute copies of Master 9–5. Help students follow the map as they listen. Play the recording several times.

9–6, 9–7 Hallelujah
Jewish Heritage Week

GRADE LEVEL: 2–5

OBJECTIVE: Students will sing and play a Hebrew song.

9–6, 9–7, Hallelujah, *continued*

MATERIALS: Masters 9–6, 9–7; bellsets or keyboards

PREPARATION: Make student copies of Masters 9–6 and 9–7.

DIRECTIONS: Distribute student copies of Master 9–6. Help students sing the song. Add leader and group parts as indicated. Divide the class into small groups of four members each. Distribute copies of Master 9–7 and instruments to each group. Allow time for groups to learn to read and play the song.

9–8 That's What Mothers Are Made of
Mother's Day, Second Sunday in May

GRADE LEVEL: 2–3

OBJECTIVE: Students will create verses for a verse-refrain song.

MATERIALS: Master 9–8; scissors, glue, tagboard, yarn, paper punch (optional)

PREPARATION: Make student copies of Master 9–8.

DIRECTIONS: Teach the refrain by rote. Invite students to choose to complete either verse two or verse three. Help students write their ideas in the blanks and improvise melodies to perform what they have written. To perform a class song, invite individuals to sing their verses, each followed by the class's refrain.

EXTENSION: Invite students to color, cut out, and glue the heart to tagboard. Cut on jagged line to separate heart pieces. Punch holes and string yarn to make Mother's Day gifts for mother and child to wear.

That's   what   moth-ers   are   made   of

9–9 Brahms's Lullaby
Johannes Brahms, May 7

GRADE LEVEL: 3–8

OBJECTIVE: Students will label traditional notation.

MATERIALS: Master 9–9

PREPARATION: Make a transparency and student copies of Master 9–9.

DIRECTIONS: Display transparency. Invite students to help you label several blanks with your choice of syllables, numerical scale degrees, or letter names of notes. When students understand how to continue, distribute student copies and allow time for individual practice. Use the transparency again to allow students to share answers and correct their work. Sing the song, using note names, scale degrees, or syllables.

9–10, 9–11 You Can't Top My Limerick
Limerick Day, May 12

GRADE LEVEL: 5–8

OBJECTIVE: Students will sing a verse-refrain limerick song. Students will create original limericks.

MATERIALS: Master 9–10.

PREPARATION: Make student copies of Master 9–10. Make a transparency and student copies of Master 9–11.

DIRECTIONS: Help students learn to speak the limericks and sing the refrain. Distribute student copies of Master 9–11. Help students create original limericks using Grid 1 or Grid 2. Encourage volunteers to share their original limericks with the class. Assemble a verse-refrain performance with students' original limericks as the verses and the class singing the refrain after each verse.

9–12, 9–13 The Stars and Stripes Forever
The Stars and Stripes Forever Day, May 14

GRADE LEVEL: 3–6

OBJECTIVE: Students will follow and complete a map of a famous march.

MATERIALS: Masters 9–12, 9–13; recording of John Philip Sousa's "The Stars and Stripes Forever"

PREPARATION: Make a transparency of Master 9–12. Make a transparency and student copies of Master 9–13.

DIRECTIONS: Display transparency of Master 9–12. Play portions of the recording and introduce students to map symbols and the musical events they represent. Help students discover events that look and sound alike. Play the recording in its entirety. Invite students to follow along as you point out events on the transparency. Distribute students copies of Master 9–13.

9–12, 9–13, The Stars and Stripes Forever, continued

Allow time for students to translate the picture map into a form map using letters of the alphabet. Encourage students to compare answers. Display transparency of Master 9–13 and fill in correct form sequence. Play the recording again and invite students to listen, following their own form maps.

ANSWER KEY: Introduce A A B B C D C´ D C˝

9–14   Brave Americans
Memorial Day

GRADE LEVEL: 4–8

OBJECTIVE: Students will perform a song with two-part harmony.

MATERIALS: Master 9–14

PREPARATION: Make student copies of Master 9–14.

DIRECTIONS: Help students learn to sing the melody of "Brave Americans." When students can sing the melody independently, help them learn the harmony part. Assign the harmony part to a small group. Put both parts together and perform the song.

9–15   Flowering Rhythms

GRADE LEVEL: 1–6

OBJECTIVE: Students will write rhythm patterns from dictation.

MATERIALS: Master 9–15; one rhythm instrument (for example, triangle)

PREPARATION: Prepare six rhythm patterns of appropriate difficulty. Make student copies of Master 9–15.

DIRECTIONS: Distribute student copies of Master 9–15. Play rhythm patterns on a rhythm instrument. Allow time after each pattern for students to write the pattern they hear. To adapt this activity for any grade level, vary the difficulty of the patterns by length and by rhythmic content. Younger students may write patterns in icons, stick notation, or other nontraditional form as appropriate for their abilities.

9–1   **May Baskets**

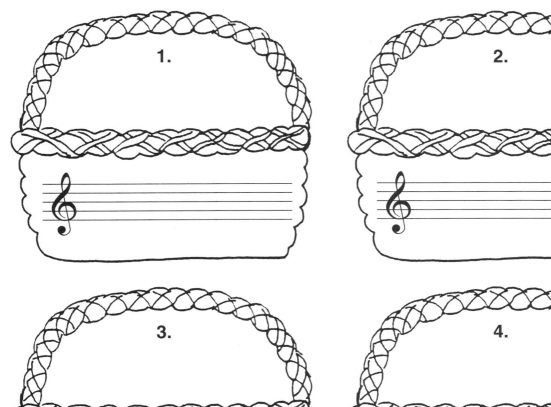

Name _____   **Date** _____

9–2   **A Tisket, A Tasket**

Directions: Read and play this song. Use these bells.

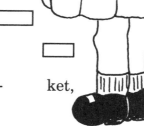

E		G		A
mi		sol		la

A - tis- ket, a - tas-   ket, a   green and yel- low   bas-   ket,

I wrote   a   let- ter   to   my   love   and   on   the way   I   dropped   it.

Fill in the missing notes on the staff below.

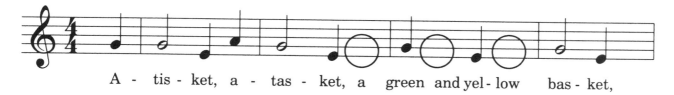

A - tis - ket, a - tas - ket, a   green and yel - low   bas - ket,

9–3　　　　　**Long-Eared Personages**

Listen to "Long-Eared
Personages." Follow
the map below as
you listen to the
high and low sounds.

9–4   **Royal March of the Lion**

roar—

9–5   **Fossils**

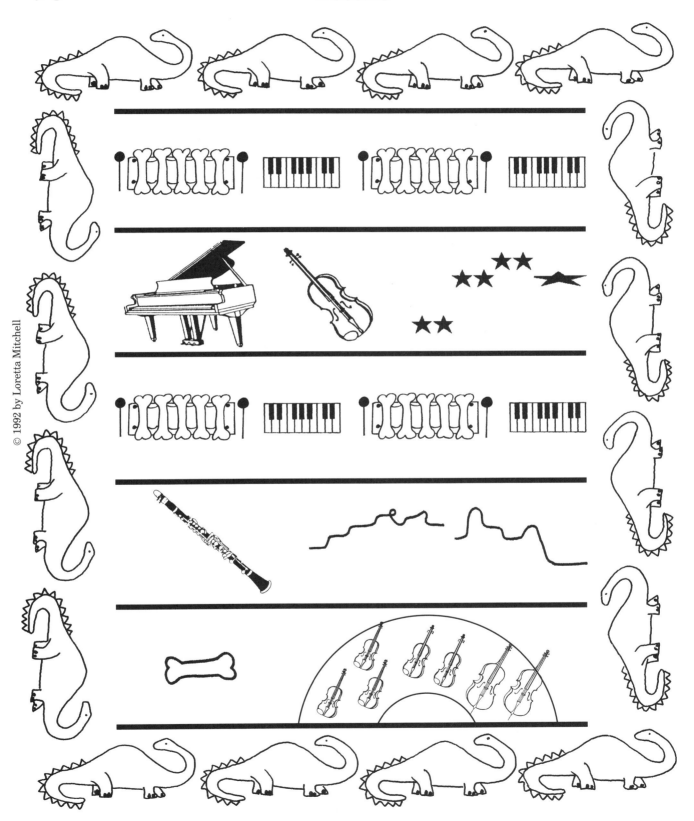

9–6

Hallelujah

Hebrew Folk Song

Hal-le-lu, Hal-le-lu, Hal-le-lu, Hal-le-lu! Sing out with joy!

Hal-le-lu, Hal-le-lu, Hal-le-lu, Hal-le-lu! Sing out with joy!

Sing out with joy, Hal-le-lu-jah! Sing out with joy, Hal-le-lu-jah!

Sing out with joy, Hal-le-lu-jah! Sing out with joy!

Name _____   Date _____

9–7   # Hallelujah

Hebrew Folk Song

Leader	**Group**
4 lu! 1 lu, Hal-le- 6 lu, Hal-le- 5, Hal-le-lu, Hal-le-	3 Sing 2 out with 1 joy!
Leader	**Group**
4 lu! 1 lu, Hal-le- 6, lu, Hal-le- 5, Hal-le-lu, Hal-le-	3 Sing 2 out with 1 joy!
Leader	**Group**
3 out 1 Sing 1 with 2 joy,	4 lu- 3 le- 2 Hal- 2 jah!
Leader	**Group**
2 out 7, Sing 7, with 1 joy,	3 lu- 2 le- 1 Hal- 1 jah!
Leader	**Group**
3 out 1 Sing 1 with 2 joy,	4 lu- 3 le- 2 Hal- 2 jah!

All
5 Sing 7, out with 1 joy!

Name _____   Date _____

9–8   **That's What Mothers Are Made of**

1. Hugs and kisses and bundles of fun.

Refrain

That's ————
         what
             moth-
                 ers   made ————
                    are   of ————

2. <u>Love and kindness and</u> _____

3. _____

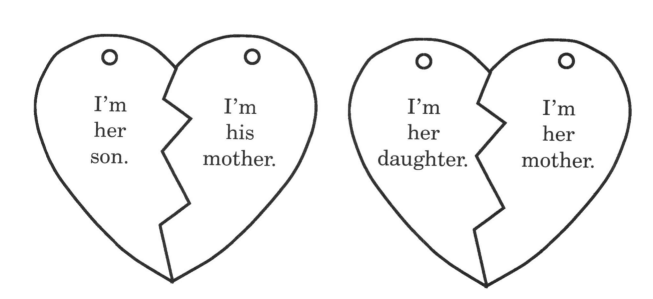

Name _____   Date _____

9–9   **Brahms's Lullaby**

by Johannes Brahms

Directions: Label these notes. Fill in the blanks with letter names, scale degrees, or syllables.

Name _____ Date _____

9–10 **You Can't Top My Limerick**

There once was a fellow from Norway,
Who said he'd invented one more way
To enter a room.
We'll only assume
He's tired of using the doorway.

Refrain

A lim'-rick, a lim'-rick, You can't top my lim'-rick,

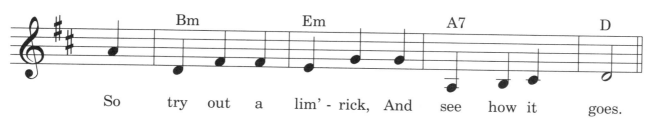

So try out a lim'-rick, And see how it goes.

A speedy young fellow named Steve
Walked faster than you can believe.
He'd start out on Sunday,
Get back home on Monday:
The Monday before he would leave.

Name _____ **Date** _____

9–11   **You Can't Top My Limerick**

1. Complete this limerick. Write one syllable in each box. Make sure that the three "A" boxes rhyme with each other. Make sure that the two "B" boxes rhyme with each other.

There	once	was	a	boy	from	St.	A Paul

Who							A

He				B	

And				B	

Be-	cause	he					A

2. Write your own limerick. Write one syllable in each box. Make sure that the three "A" boxes rhyme with each other. Make sure that the two "B" boxes rhyme with each other.

							A

							A

			B	

			B	

						A

© 1992 by Loretta Mitchell

Name _____ Date _____

9–12   # The Stars and Stripes Forever
by John Philip Sousa

Directions: Listen to a famous march. Follow this map.

INTRODUCTION

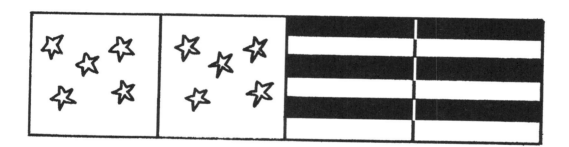

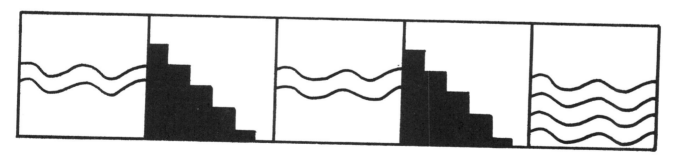

Listening map adapted from original map by Gloria Kiester, St, Olaf College, Northfield, MN 55057. Used by permission

Name _____ Date _____

9–13 # The Stars and Stripes Forever
by John Philip Sousa

Directions: Listen to "The Stars and Stripes Forever." Fill in this blank map with letters of the alphabet to show the form of the march.

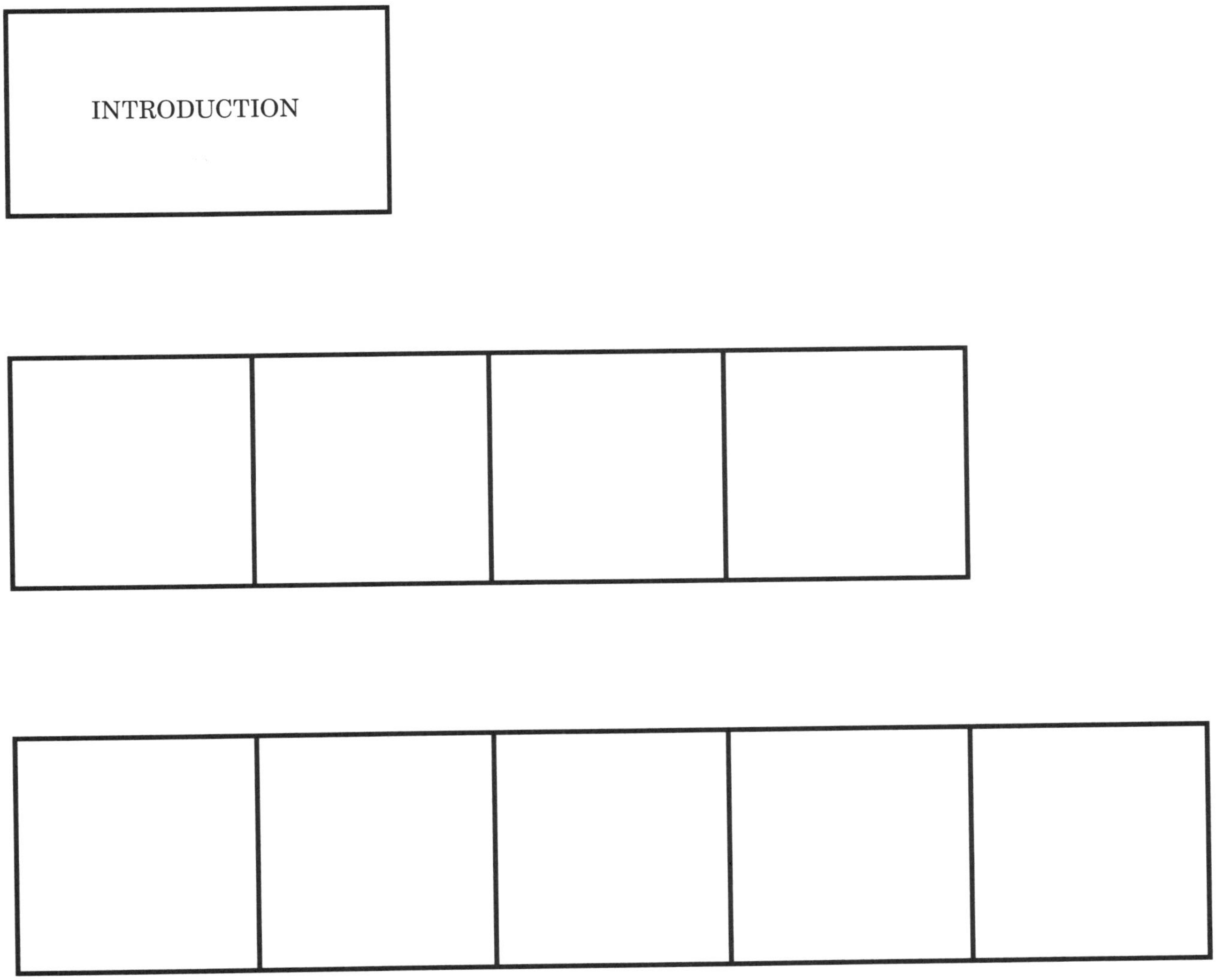

INTRODUCTION

Name _____ **Date** _____

9–14

Brave Americans

Directions: Learn to sing this song.

Scores of young Am - er - i - cans   fought for lib - er - ty,

Brave - ly sac - ri - ficed their lives to   keep our coun-try   free.

2. How can we say thank you
   For the price they had to pay?
   Father, bless their memory,
   We honor them today.

Add a harmony part:

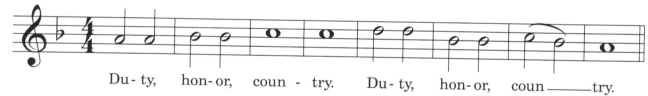

Du - ty,   hon - or,   coun - try.   Du - ty,   hon - or,   coun ——— try.

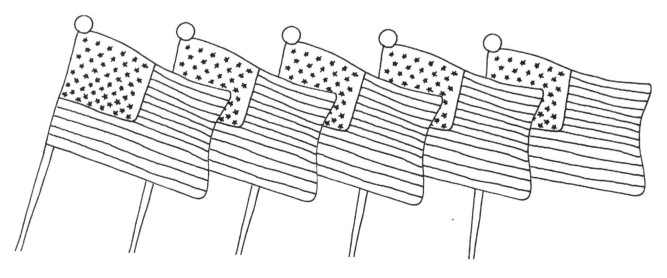

Name _____   **Date** _____

9–15   **Flowering Rhythms**

1.

2.

3.

4.

5.

6.

10–1 Dive on in, the Water's Fine!

GRADE LEVEL: 1–5

OBJECTIVE: Students will write rhythm patterns from dictation.

MATERIALS: Master 10–1; one rhythm instrument (for example, triangle)

PREPARATION: Prepare five rhythm patterns of appropriate difficulty. Make student copies of Master 10–1.

DIRECTIONS: Distribute student copies of Master 10–1. Play rhythm patterns on a rhythm instrument. Allow time after each pattern for students to write the pattern they hear. To adapt this activity for any grade level, vary the difficulty of the patterns by length and by rhythmic content. Younger students may write patterns in icons, stick notation, or other nontraditional form as appropriate for their abilities.

10-2 Thank You, Teachers
Teacher Thank You Week

GRADE LEVEL: 2–4

OBJECTIVE: Students will improvise melodies and perform a call-and-response song.

MATERIALS: Master 10–2; resonator bells

PREPARATION: Make a transparency of Master 10–2.

DIRECTIONS: Say these words for the class to echo.

> Thank   you   teach - ers

Encourage students to create a four-note melody for the words. Try several students' melodies. Use class consensus to choose a melody and write it on the transparency in the boxes or on the staff. Help students improvise spoken lines about their teachers (for example, "For helping us learn to read"). Encourage them to improvise melodies for their phrases. After each addition, the class will respond with "Thank you, teachers."

10–3 A Father's Day Song
Father's Day, Third Sunday in June

GRADE LEVEL: 2–4

OBJECTIVE: Students will compose a song about their fathers.

MATERIALS: Master 10–3; bellsets

PREPARATION: Make a transparency and student copies of Master 10–3.

DIRECTIONS: Review student instructions with the class. Allow time for students to compose. Encourage students to perform their compositions for the class.

10–4 Hooray, Hooray!
End of School

GRADE LEVEL: 1–3

OBJECTIVE: Students will improvise verses for a cumulative verse-refrain song.

MATERIALS: Master 10–4

PREPARATION: Make a transparency of Master 10–4.

DIRECTIONS: Help students learn to sing the refrain. Invite students to create their own endings for the "Time for _____" verse. Help them improvise melodies for their verses. Choose a volunteer to share his or her verse with the class. Add the class refrain after the verse. Add a second verse, and so forth.

EXTENSION: (1) Add a clap/snap pattern to accompany the song. (2) Make the song cumulative by "saving solos." For example, soloist #1 sings "Time for playing." After the second refrain, soloist #2 sings "Time for Picnics"; then soloist #1 sings "Time for playing." After the third refrain, three soloists improvise, and so forth.

10–5 Hopping from Form to Form

GRADE LEVEL: 3–5

OBJECTIVE: Students will identify musical forms.

MATERIALS: Master 10–5; recorded examples of musical forms: AB, ABA, AABA, theme and variations, rondo

PREPARATION: Make student copies of Master 10–5.

*10-5, **Hopping from Form to Form**, continued*

DIRECTIONS: Distribute student copies. Play the first recorded example. Instruct students to identify the form and write a number 1 on the correct lily pad. Compare student responses, correct answers and replay the example. Continue with other examples.

10–6 Catch a fish

GRADE LEVEL: 2–5

OBJECTIVE: Students will read and identify treble clef notation.

MATERIALS: Master 10–6; one keyboard or bellset

PREPARATION: Prepare six melody patterns of appropriate difficulty. Notate the patterns on Master 10–6. Make student copies of Master 10–6.

DIRECTIONS: Distribute student copies of Master 10–6. Play (or sing) melodic pattern #1. Allow time for students to find the pattern on their copies. Instruct students to label the notes in the pattern and sing it back to you. Continue with the other five patterns.

10–1   # Dive on in, the Water's Fine!

Directions: Listen to the patterns your teacher plays. Write what you hear in the spaces below.

_____

1.

2.

3.

4.

5.

Name _____   Date _____

10–2   **Thank You, Teachers**

Compose a melody for these words.
Use these bells:

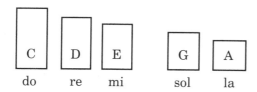

| C | D | E | G | A |
| do | re | mi | sol | la |

Write one letter in each box.

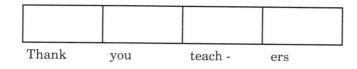

Thank   you   teach -   ers

Write your melody on the staff.

Thank   you   teach –   ers

Complete this phrase:

For _____

Make up a melody for your phrase. Share your phrase with the class.

Put the song together:

Solo: For _____   Class: Thank you, teachers

Solo: For _____   Class: Thank you, teachers

Solo: For _____   Class: Thank you, teachers

Solo: For _____   Class: Thank you, teachers

Name _____   **Date** _____

10–3   **A Father's Day Song**

Directions: Compose a Father's Day song.
Use these bells.

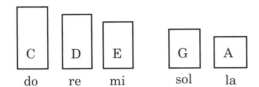

Write one letter in each box.
Sing and play your song.

I	wish	you	a	hap -	py	Fath -	er's	Day.

Fath -	er's	Day,	Fath-	er's	Day.

I	wish	you	a	hap -	py	Fath -	er's	Day.

'Cuz	I	love	you.

Name _____ Date _____

10–4 **Hooray, Hooray!**

Class:

Hoo - ray, Hoo - ray! What can we say?

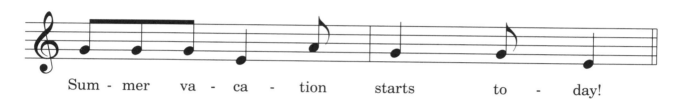

Sum - mer va - ca - tion starts to - day!

Solo:
Time for ___ (playing) ___

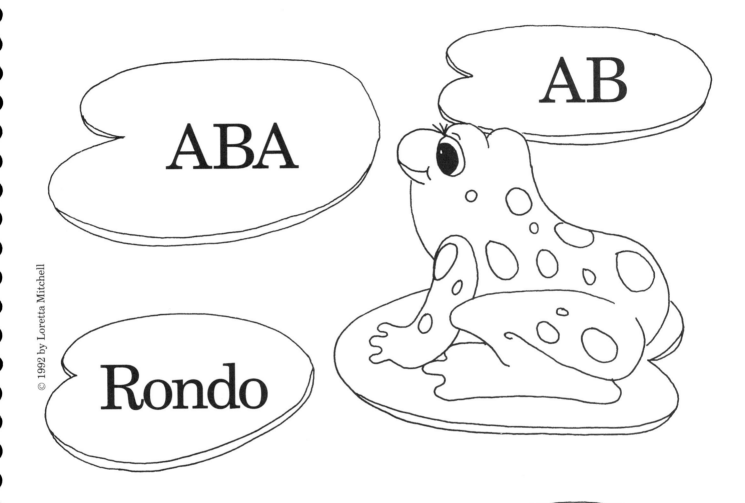

10–6   **Catch a Fish**

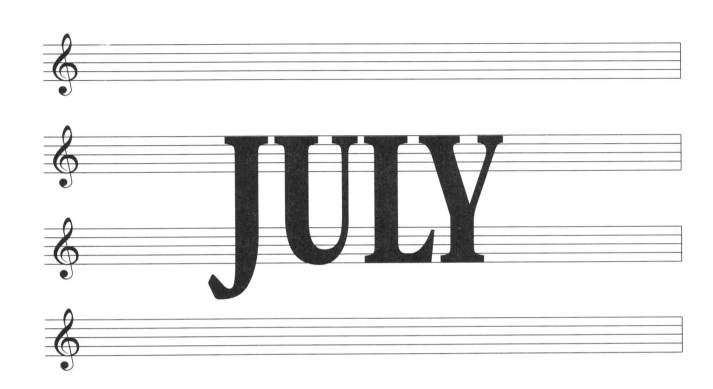

207

JULY
TEACHER'S GUIDE

11–1 Have a Picnic!

GRADE LEVEL: 3–5

OBJECTIVE: Students will identify musical forms.

MATERIALS: Master 11–1; recorded examples of musical forms: AB, ABA, AABA, verse-refrain, theme and variations, rondo

PREPARATION: Make student copies of Master 11–1.

DIRECTIONS: Distribute student copies. Play an ABA example. Instruct students to find a picture that matches what they heard and label it ABA. Compare student responses, correct answers, and replay the example. Continue with five other examples in any sequence you choose.

11–2 Who Is Satchmo?
Louis Armstrong, July 4

GRADE LEVEL: 5–8

OBJECTIVE: Students will understand Louis Armstrong's contribution to jazz and listen to a Louis Armstrong recording.

MATERIALS: Master 11–2; recording of "Hello, Dolly" or other Armstrong recording

PREPARATION: Make a copy of Master 11–2.

DIRECTIONS: Introduce the music of Louis Armstrong by playing a recording. Distribute student copies. Assign a research project with a specific due date. Instruct students to find answers to questions 1 to 5 on the page. Compare answers and discuss other information that students found interesting in their research. Replay the recording and answer questions 6 and 7.

11–3, 11–4 This Land Is Your Land
Woody Guthrie, July 14

GRADE LEVEL: 4–6

MATERIALS: Masters 11–3, 11–4; alto glockenspiel, alto metallophone, bass xylophone

OBJECTIVE: Students will sing a two-part song with instrumental accompaniment.

PREPARATION: Make student copies of the song, Master 11–3. Make a transparency of Master 11–4.

DIRECTIONS: Teach or review the song, "This Land Is Your Land." When students can sing it well, help students learn to play the instrumental parts (Master 11–4). Add instrument parts one at a time. Help students learn to sing the harmony part. Add it to the song and the accompaniment. Encourage student suggestions for creating an introduction and a coda.

11–5 Yankee Doodle
Independence Day, July 4

GRADE LEVEL: 1–4

OBJECTIVE: Students will read iconic and symbolic notation.

MATERIALS: Master 11–5; bellsets; mallets; pencils

PREPARATION: Make a transparency and student copies of Master 11–5.

DIRECTIONS: Determine whether students will work individually or in small groups. Distribute student copies. Allow time for students to read the icons and play the song. Help students complete the symbolic notation at the bottom of the page.

11–6 Teddy Bear, Teddy Bear
All-American Teddy Bear's Picnic

GRADE LEVEL: K–2

OBJECTIVE: Students will follow melodic icons.

MATERIALS: Master 11–6

11–6, Teddy Bear, Teddy Bear, continued

PREPARATION: Make a transparency and student copies of Master 11–6.

DIRECTIONS: Teach the song by rote. Display transparency. Follow icons as the class sings. Distribute student copies. Invite students to trace the icons as they chant.

s   s   m   s   s   m   s   l   s   m
Teddy Bear, Teddy Bear, turn around,

s   s   m   s   s   m   s   m   r
Teddy Bear, Teddy Bear, touch the ground.

s   s   m   s   s   m   s   l   s   m
Teddy Bear, Teddy Bear, tie your shoe.

s   s   m   s   s   m   s   m   d
Teddy Bear, Teddy Bear, that will do.

11–7 Singing Telegram
A Singing Telegram Birthday, July 28

GRADE LEVEL: 4–8

OBJECTIVE: Students will create singing telegrams.

MATERIALS: Master 11–7

PREPARATION: Make a transparency and student copies of Master 11–7. Create a singing telegram to use as a model, for example, a birthday telegram to the tune of "Twinkle, Twinkle, Little Star."

> It's your birthday, yes it's true,
> Have a party, maybe two!
> Open presents, sing a song,
> Celebrate the whole day long.
> Count the candles, have some fun.
> Tell the world you're twenty-one!

DIRECTIONS: Distribute student copies. Clarify the instructions if necessary. Fill in the transparency with the choices you used to create your telegram. Demonstrate your singing telegram. Allow time for students to work. Encourage volunteers to share their telegrams with the class.

11–8, 11–9 What Baseball's About

GRADE LEVEL: 2–4

OBJECTIVE: Students will perform a chant with rhythmic accompaniment.

MATERIALS: Masters 11–8, 11–9; rhythm instruments

PREPARATION: Make transparencies of Masters 11–8 and 11–9.

DIRECTIONS: Display transparency 11–8. Help students learn the chant. Display transparency 11–9. Help students read and clap the rhythms. Distribute rhythm instruments. Rehearse the parts separately and then sequence them according to the transparency. Add the accompaniment to the chant. Invite students to exchange instruments and try the accompaniment again.

11–10 Catch a Fly

GRADE LEVEL: 5–7

OBJECTIVE: Students will read and identify bass clef notation.

MATERIALS: Master 11–10; keyboard

PREPARATION: Prepare six melody patterns of appropriate difficulty. Notate the patterns on Master 11–10. Make student copies of Master 11–10.

DIRECTIONS: Distribute student copies of Master 11–10. Play (or sing) melodic pattern #1. Allow time for students to find the pattern on their copies. Instruct students to label the notes in the pattern and sing it back to you. Continue with the other five patterns.

11–1   **Have a Picnic!**

Directions: Listen to musical examples. Find the picture that matches each form. Label each picture.

CHOICES		
AB	ABA	AABA
Verse-Refrain	Theme and Variations	Rondo

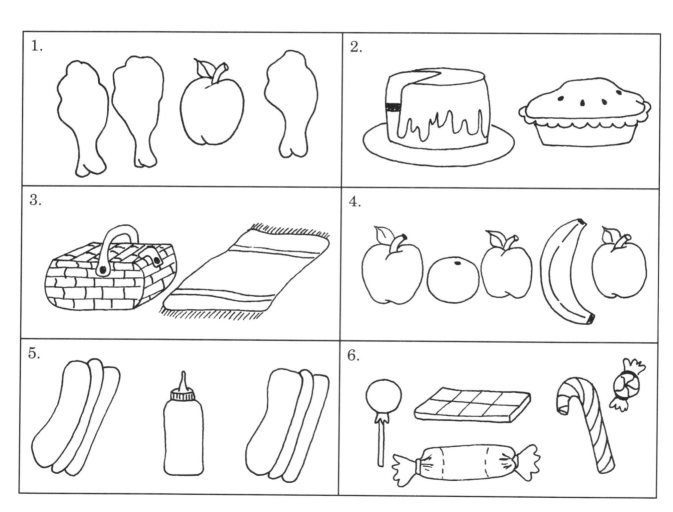

Name _____   Date _____

11–2   **Who Is Satchmo?**

Directions: Find information on a musician named Louis Armstrong. Answer

questions 1 to 7. This assignment is due _____.

1. Louis Armstrong's nickname was _____.

2. Louis Armstrong played the _____.

3. Louis Armstrong's band was known as _____

     _____ Louis Armstrong Trio   _____ The Hot Five

     _____ The Armstrong Four   _____ King Louis and His Band

4. Louis Armstrong's early lessons were given to him by _____

     _____ King Oliver   _____ Benny Goodman

     _____ Jelly Roll Morton   _____ His own father

5. Louis Armstrong introduced a style of singing. Name the style. _____.

   Describe this style of singing. _____

   _____

Listen to a Louis Armstrong recording.

6. Write the name of the song. _____

7. What musical qualities make it different from any other music you may have heard?

   _____

   _____

Name _____   Date _____

11–3   **This Land Is Your Land**

Words and Music by Woody Guthrie

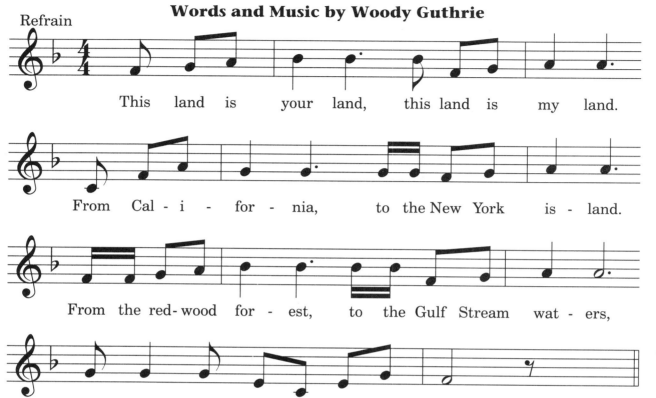

This land is your land, this land is my land.

From Cal - i - for - nia, to the New York is - land.

From the red-wood for - est, to the Gulf Stream wat - ers,

This land was made for you and me.

1. As I was walking that ribbon of highway
   I saw above me that endless skyway,
   I saw below me that golden valley,
   This land was made for you and me.
   (Refrain)

2. I've roamed and rambled
      and I followed my footsteps
   To the sparkling sands of
      her diamond deserts,
   And all around me
      a voice was sounding,
   This land was made for you and me.
   (Refrain)

3. When the sun came shining
      and I was strolling
   And the wheat fields waving
      and the dust clouds rolling,
   As the fog was lifting,
      a voice was chanting,
   This land was made for you and me.
   (Refrain)

Name _____   Date _____

11–4   # This Land Is Your Land

Words and Music by Woody Guthrie

Directions: Sing "This Land Is Your Land." Add these instrument parts to the song.

Alto Glockenspiel

Alto Xylophone

Bass Xylophone

Learn to sing this harmony part. Choose a small group of students to sing this part. Add it to the song.

la la   la la   la la   la la   la la   la la la   la———

Instrumental accompaniments by Jane Frazee, Director, University of St. Thomas Institute for Contemporary Music Education.

Name _____   **Date** _____

11–5   **Yankee Doodle**

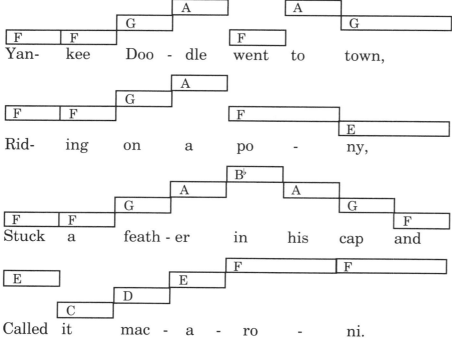

Yan- kee Doo - dle went to town,

Rid- ing on a po - ny,

Stuck a feath - er in his cap and

Called it mac - a - ro - ni.

Fill in the missing notes.

Yan- kee Doo- dle went to town,

Rid - ing on a po - ny,

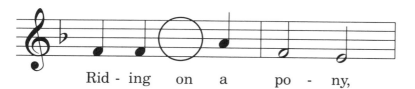

Stuck a feath- er in his cap and

Called it mac - a - ro - ni.

Name _____   Date _____

11–6   **Teddy Bear, Teddy Bear**

Ted - dy   Ted - dy   Turn   a -
                                            ro
Bear,   Bear,   u
                                                nd

Ted - dy   Ted - dy   Touch
Bear,   Bear,   the
                                ground.

                                            your
Ted - dy   Ted - dy   Tie   sh
Bear,   Bear,   o
                                               e

Ted - dy   Ted - dy   That
Bear,   Bear,   will
                                do.

Name _____ **Date** _____

11–7   **A Singing Telegram**

Directions: Create your own singing telegram. Follow the steps below.

1. Choose a person who will receive the telegram. _____ Mother _____ Father _____ Sister _____ Brother _____ Friend _____ _____	2. Choose an occasion. _____ Birthday _____ Anniversary _____ Valentine's Day _____ Spring _____ _____
3. Choose a familiar tune. _____ Yankee Doodle _____ Twinkle, Twinkle, Little Star _____ Mary Had a Little Lamb _____ _____	4. Write the original words to the song you chose. Use the back of this page.
5. Change the words to send a special telegram message. Use the back of this page.	6. Practice singing your telegram.
7. Plan how you will deliver your telegram. _____ Where? _____ _____ When? _____ _____ Will you wear a costume?	8. Deliver your telegram. How did the person react?

11–8   **What Baseball's About**

3/4 ♩ ♩ ♩ | ♩ ♩ | ♩ ♩ ♩ | ♩. |
Give me a hel - met, give me a bat.

♩ ♩ ♩ | ♩ ♩ | ♩ ♩ ♩ | ♩. |
Pitch me a curve ball, I can hit that!

♩ ♩ ♩ | ♩ ♩ | ♩ ♩ ♩ | ♩. |
Pitch me a fast ball, Can't strike me out.

♩ ♩ ♩ | ♩ ♩ ♩ | ♩ ♩ ♩ | ♩. ‖
Play- ing for fun is what base-ball's a - bout.

11–9   **What Baseball's About**

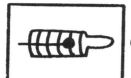 Give

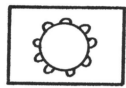 Pitch

 Pitch

 Playing

11–10   **Catch A Fly**

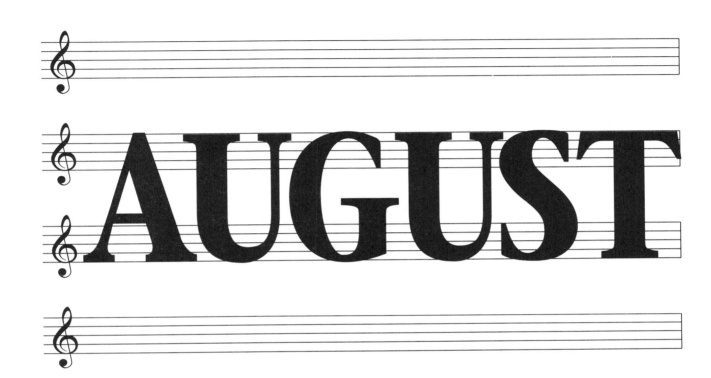

223

AUGUST
TEACHER'S GUIDE

12–1, 12–2 I'm a Clown
National Clown Week

GRADE LEVEL: 3–6

OBJECTIVE: Students will compose and notate one phrase of a song. Students will conduct a song in triple meter.

MATERIALS: Masters 12–1, 12–2; keyboards, recorders, or bellsets

PREPARATION: Make a transparency and student copies of Master 12–1. Make a transparency of Master 12–2.

DIRECTIONS: Display transparency 12–1. Help students learn to sing the first three lines of the song. Distribute student copies. Clarify the directions if necessary. Allow time for students to compose. Encourage individuals to share their ideas with the class. Use group consensus to select one idea to notate on transparency 12–1. Display transparency 12–2. Help the class transfer letter notation to traditional notation on transparency 12–2. Direct students' attention to the "Conducting in Three's" diagram. Demonstrate conducting in three's. Allow time for students to practice. Lead the class as they sing and conduct the song.

12–3 Sing and Conduct

GRADE LEVEL: 4–8

OBJECTIVE: Students will conduct songs in two's, three's, and four's.

MATERIALS: Master 12–3

PREPARATION: Make student copies of Master 12–3.

DIRECTIONS: Distribute student copies. Help students select and sing one song from the page. Demonstrate the correct conducting pattern for the song. Sing the song again and help students conduct as they sing. Continue with other songs and conducting patterns.

12–4, 12–5 Music of the Sitar
India Independence Day, August 15

GRADE LEVEL: 4–8

OBJECTIVE: Students will listen to sitar music and discuss the sitar. Students will match terms with their definitions.

MATERIALS: Masters 12–4, 12–5; recording of sitar music (for example, Ravi Shankar)

PREPARATION: Make student copies of Masters 12–4 and 12–5.

DIRECTIONS: Distribute student copies. Play a recording of sitar music. Using Master 12–4, introduce and discuss terms associated with the sitar. Invite students to match terms on Master 12–5. Compare and correct answers. Relisten to the sitar recording.

12–6 Discovering Impressionism
Claude Debussy, August 22

GRADE LEVEL: 6–8

OBJECTIVE: Students will compare elements in impressionistic painting and impressionistic music.

MATERIALS: Master 12–6; recording of Claude Debussy's "Clair de Lune"; art print: Auguste Renoir's *The Boating Party*

PREPARATION: Make student copies of Master 12–6.

DIRECTIONS: Review musical elements (rhythm, melody, harmony, timbre, form, expressive elements) and visual art elements (color, value, shape, space, texture, balance). Introduce "Clair de Lune." Distribute student copies. Invite students to discover Debussy's uses of musical elements and write their thoughts in spaces provided. Introduce *The Boating Party*. Invite students to discover Renoir's uses of design elements and to write their thoughts in spaces provided. Direct students' attention to questions 3 and 4 at the bottom of the page. Begin a class discussion about the similarities between the painting and the music example. Relisten to the music and restudy the print as many times as necessary.

12–7 The Ants Go Marching

GRADE LEVEL: 3–4

MATERIALS: Master 12–7; resonator bells

12–7, The Ants Go Marching, continued

OBJECTIVE: Students will add harmony to a song.

PREPARATION: Make a transparency of Master 12–7.

DIRECTIONS: Teach or review the song, "The Ants Go Marching." Distribute resonator bells. Help students learn to follow the chord chart, Master 12–7. Practice playing the chords tremolo style, individually and then in sequence. Add the bell accompaniment to the song. Encourage students to share additional verses they know with the class.

12–8 Tennis, Anyone?

GRADE LEVEL: 2–5

OBJECTIVE: Students will read, sing, and play treble clef notation.

MATERIALS: Master 12–8; keyboards or bellsets

PREPARATION: Prepare six melody patterns of appropriate difficulty. Notate the patterns on Master 12–8. Make student copies of Master 12–8.

DIRECTIONS: Distribute student copies of Master 12–8. Play (or sing) melodic pattern #1. Allow time for students to find the pattern on their copies. Instruct students to label the notes in the pattern and sing it back to you. Continue with the other five patterns. Distribute bellsets. Repeat the exercise with students playing each pattern as they find it on their copies.

12–9 Canoeing Fun

GRADE LEVEL: 1–6

OBJECTIVE: Students will read and play rhythmic patterns.

MATERIALS: Master 12–9; rhythm instruments

PREPARATION: Prepare six rhythm patterns of appropriate difficulty. Notate the patterns on Master 12–9. Make student copies of Master 12–9.

DIRECTIONS: Distribute student copies of Master 12–9. Play rhythm pattern #1. Allow time for students to find the pattern on their copies and place a "1" in the box. Continue with patterns 2 to 6. Distribute rhythm instruments. Allow time for students to learn to play the patterns. Repeat rhythm patterns. As you play a pattern, invite students to identify the pattern and play it back to you.

12–10 Back to School

GRADE LEVEL: 2–4

OBJECTIVE: Students will match icons and rhythmic notation.

MATERIALS: Master 12–10

PREPARATION: Make student copies of Master 12–10.

DIRECTIONS: Invite students to name supplies they need to start a new school year. Notate rhythms of suggested items. Distribute student copies. Instruct students to match the icons with the rhythm patterns. Compare and correct answers.

12–1   # I'm a Clown

Directions: Compose a melody for the last line of this song. Use a recorder, a keyboard, or these bells.

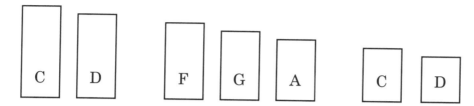

| C | D | | F | G | A | | C | D |

Write one letter in each box.

C	G	G	G	A	A	A	G	E	C	D
I	make	up	my	face	with	a	smile	or	a	frown,

C	G	G	G	A	G	E	D	D	D	G
My	pol-	ka-	dot	trous-	ers	may	seem	to	fall	down,

C	G	G	G	A	A	A	G	E	C	D
My	mag-	i-	cal	flow-	ers,	my	tri-	cy-	cle	too.

Be -	cause	I'm	a	clown,	I'll	en-	ter-	tain	you.

Name _____   **Date** _____

12–2   # I'm a Clown

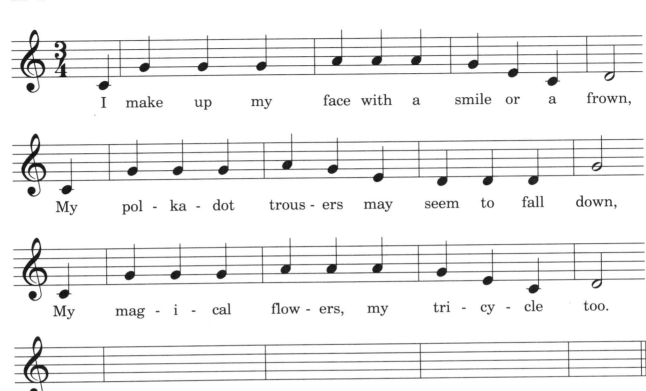

I make up my face with a smile or a frown,

My pol - ka - dot trous - ers may seem to fall down,

My mag - i - cal flow - ers, my tri - cy - cle too.

Be - cause I'm a clown, I'll en - ter - tain you.

Conducting in Three's

12–3

Sing and Conduct

IN TWO'S

She'll be Comin' 'Round the Mountain
Skip to My Lou
Hush, Little Baby
London Bridge Is Falling Down
This Old Man
The Bear Went Over the Mountain
Old MacDonald Had a Farm
Row, Row, Row Your Boat
The Angel Band
Oh! Susanna

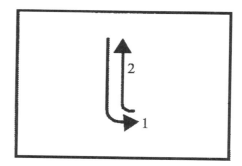

IN THREE'S

There's a Hole in the Bucket
Bicycle Built for Two
The Man on the Flying Trapeze
We Wish You a Merry Christmas
Du, Du, Liegst Mir im Herzen
America
On Top of Old Smoky

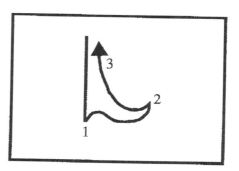

IN FOUR'S

If You're Happy and You Know It
Little Cabin in the Wood
B-I-N-G-O
John Jacob Jingleheimerschmidt
Are You Sleeping?
The Hokey Pokey
Baa Baa Black Sheep
I've Been Working on the Railroad
America the Beautiful
Alouette

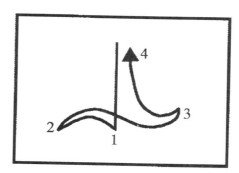

12–4 **Music of the Sitar**

Directions: Listen to music of the sitar. Discuss these terms with your class.

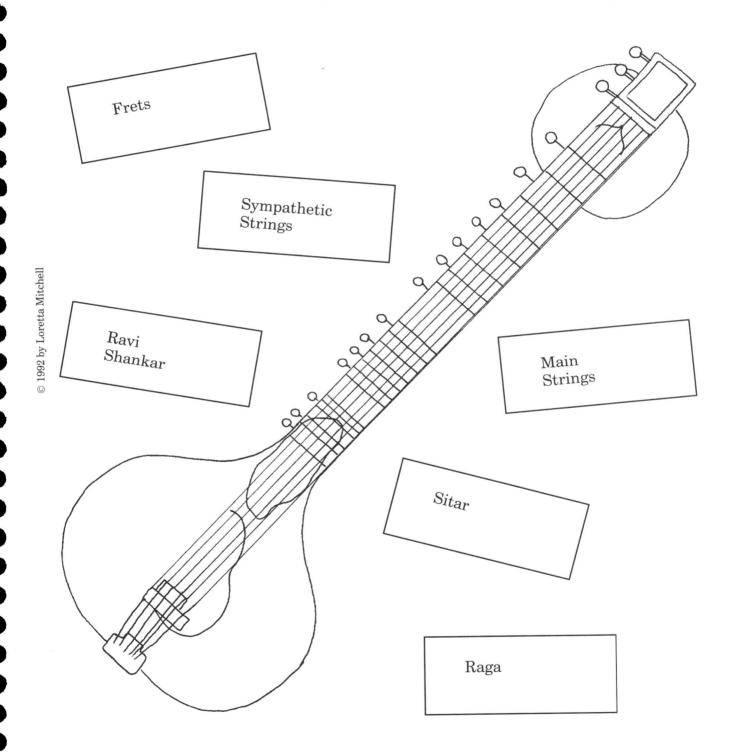

Frets

Sympathetic
Strings

Ravi
Shankar

Main
Strings

Sitar

Raga

12–5   **Music of the Sitar**

Directions: Listen to music of the sitar. Discuss these terms with your class. Match the terms with the definitions.

1. | Sitar |

| seven strings plucked by the sitar player |

2. | Sympathetic Strings |

| stringed instrument with long neck, strings, and frets |

3. | Raga |

| finger guides or bands on the neck of the sitar |

4. | Main Strings |

| strings under the main strings; vibrate when main strings are plucked |

5. | Frets |

| music played on a sitar |

6. | Ravi Shankar |

| a famous sitar player |

Name _____   Date _____

Discovering Impressionism

1. Listen to "Clair de Lune." Decide how these elements of music were used by the composer.

   ♪ Rhythm _____

   ♪ Melody _____

   ♪ Harmony _____

   ♪ Form _____

   ♪ Timbre _____

   ♪ Expressive Elements _____

2. Study *The Boating Party* by Renoir. Decide how these elements of design were used by the artist.

   Color _____

   Value _____

   Shape _____

   Space _____

   Texture _____

   Balance _____

3. Compare the painting and the music. Which elements are similar?

   _____

   _____

4. Which elements suggest that these works of art were created about the same time in history?

   _____

   _____

Name _____   **Date** _____

12–7   **The Ants Go Marching**

Directions: Distribute these bells. Divide your class into chord groups.

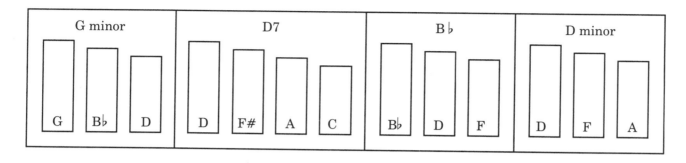

G minor	D7	B♭	D minor
G B♭ D	D F# A C	B♭ D F	D F A

1. Sing these words to the tune "When Johnny Comes Marching Home." Use chord groups to accompany the song.

   Key of G minor

        Gm   B♭
   The ants go marching one by one, hurrah, hurrah.

        Gm   B♭   D7
   The ants go marching one by one, hurrah, hurrah.

        Gm   D7
   The ants go marching one by one,

        Gm   D7
   The little one stops to have some fun,

        Gm   D7   Gm   Dm   Gm
   And they all come marching down to get out of the rain.

2. Do you know other verses for this song?

   The ants go marching two by two, hurrah, hurrah.
   The ants go marching two by two, hurrah, hurrah.
   The ants go marching two by two,
   The little one stops to _____,
   And they all come marching down to get out of the rain.

   The ants go marching three by three, hurrah, hurrah. . . .

Name _____   Date _____

12–8   **Tennis, Anyone?**

Directions: Name the notes in each of these patterns. Play the patterns on a keyboard or bellset.

1.

2.

3.

4.

5.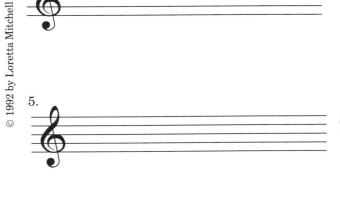

6.

Name _____   Date _____

12–9   **Canoeing Fun**

Directions: Your teacher will play rhythm patterns on an instrument. Find each pattern and place the correct number in the box.

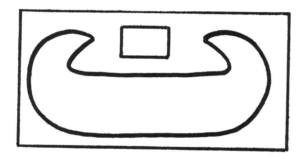 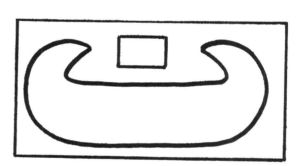

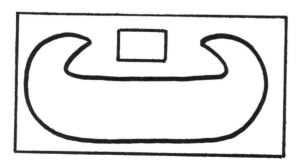 

12–10   **Back to School**

Directions: These are supplies you will need to start school. Match the icons on the left with the rhythm patterns on the right.

1. box of crayons
   □ □ □ □

2. pencil box
   □ □ ▭

3. scissors
   ▭ ▭

4. paste
   ▭

5. backpack
   ▭ ▭

6. lunch money
   ▭ □ □

INDEXES

ALPHABETICAL INDEX OF TITLES

Aaron Copland Hall of Fame, 3–7
Admission: One Ticket, 1–5
American Composers, 3–2
Ants Go Marching, The, 12–7
April Fool, 8–1, 8–2
A Tisket, A Tasket, 9–2
Back to School, 12–10
Black and Gold, 2–14, 2–15
Brahms Lullaby, 9–9
Brave Americans, 9–14
Bushels of Apples, 2–1
Canoe Song, 1–10
Canoe Song, 1–11
Canoeing Fun, 12–9
Catch a Fish, 10–1
Catch a Fly, 11–10
Caught in a Spider Web, 2–17, 2–18, 2–19
Celebrate Music Education, 7–1
Christmas Carol Challenge, 4–8
Christopher Columbus, 2–3
Contrasts, 5–4
Counting Acorns, 1–8
Discovering Impressionism, 12–6
Dive On In, the Water's Fine!, 10–2
Doo Dah Doo Dah, 5–9
Dot Dot Dot Dash, 4–3
Easter Egg Hunt, 8–9, 8–10
Extra! Extra! Our School is Great!, 3–1
Father's Day Song, A, 10–4
February Melodies, 6–11
Figure Eight Forms, 5–7
Flowering Rhythms, 9–15
Fossils, 9–5
Give a Cheer, 1–6
Grandmas Are Like That, 1–1
Grandpas Are Like That, 1–2
Gunpowder Run, 5–12, 5–13
Hallelujah Chorus, 4–11
Hallelujah, 9–6, 9–7
Halloween Rondo, 2–20, 2–21
Hanukkah, 4–4
Happy Birthday, Dear Sebastian, 7–10, 7–1
Have a Picnic, 11–1
Hello, How Are You? 7–6
Holiday Rhythms, 4–7
Hooray! Hooray! 10–5
Hopping From Form to Form, 10–6
I Love to Read, 8–4
I'm a Clown, 12–1, 12–2
Invent a Musical Instrument, 6–3

It's Raining, 8–12
It's Time to Turn to Spring, 8–5
Jingle Bells, 4–9, 4–10
Johnny Appleseed, 7–7
Let's Go Fly a Kite, 7–14
Lions and Lambs, 7–13
Little Fugue in G Minor, 7–9
Little Orphant Annie, 2–10, 2–11
Long–Eared Personages, 9–3
Love Somebody, 6–6
Love Somebody, 6–7
Love to Me, Love to You, 6–4, 6–5
Lovely Rhythms, 6–10
Make Your Own String Instrument, 4–6
Maple Leaf Rag, 3–9
Martin, 5–5
May Baskets, 9–1
Minute Waltz, The, 6–8
Music Trivia, 5–3
Music of the Sitar, 12–4, 12–5
Names and Faces, 1–12
New Year's Chords, 5–2
Nine Lives, 2–12, 2–13
Nutcracker, The, 4–13
O'er the Ramparts, 7–4
On the First Thanksgiving, 3–10
Over the River and Through the Wood, 3–12
Paddy Works on the Railway, 7–8
Peanuts Peanuts Peanuts, 7–2
Peter and the Wolf, 8–7, 8–8
Pizza for All, 5–6
Popping, Popping, 2–2
Raking Leaves, 1–13
Rhapsody in Blue, 1–9
Royal March of the Lion, 9–4
Sandwich Music, 3–3
Saxophones and Their Cousins, 3–4
Sempre Fidelis, 3–5
Sempre Fidelis, 3–6
Sing and Conduct, 12–3
Sing of Peace, 1–3, 1–4
Singing Telegram, A, 11–7
Song for the New Year, A, 5–1
Songs from Around the World, 2–7, 2–8
Sounds of Autumn, 1–7
Star Spangled Melody, A, 7–5
Stars and Stripes Forever, The, 9–12, 9–13
Surprise Symphony, 7–12
Swing Era, The, 7–3
Symphony No. 40, 5–8

Symphony No. Five, 4–2
Take Care of Your Grin, 6–1
Teddy Bear, Teddy Bear, 11–6
Ten Little Costumes, 2–9
Tennis, Anyone? 12–8
Thank You, Lord, 3–11
Thank You, Teachers, 10–3
That's What Mothers Are Made Of, 9–8
They Call It Barbershop, 8–3
This Land is Your Land, 11–3, 11–4
Three Billy Goats Gruff, 2–6
Trick or Treat, 2–16
Trout, The, 5–10, 5–11
Turkey Shoot, 3–13

Unsquare Dance, 4-1
Variations on a Familiar Carol, 4-12
Violins and How They Work, 4-5
Welcome Springtime, 8-11
What Baseball's About, 11-8, 11-9
What Do We Plant When We Plant the Tree? 8–6
Who Stowed Away? 2-4, 2-5
Will We Have More Winter? 6-2
William Tell Overture, 6-10
Windy Days of March, 7-15
Yankee Doodle, 11-5
You Can't Top My Limerick, 9-10, 9-11
Young Person's Guide to the Orchestra, 3-8

COMPOSERS

American Composers, 3–2
Bach Little Fugue in G Minor, 7–9
Bach Happy Birthday, Dear Sebastian, 7–10, 7–1
Beethoven Symphony No. Five, 4–2
Brahms Brahms Lullaby, 9–9
Britten Young Person's Guide to the Orchestra, 12–8
Brubeck Unsquare Dance, 4–1
Chopin Minute Waltz, The, 6–8
Copland Aaron Copland Hall of Fame, 3–7
Debussy Discovering Impressionism, 12–6

Foster Doo Dah Doo Dah, 5–9
Gershwin Rhapsody in Blue, 1–9
Guthrie This Land Is Your Land, 11–3, 11–4
Haydn Surprise Symphony, 7–12
Joplin Maple Leaf Rag, 3–9
Mozart Symphony No. 40, 5–8
Prokofiev Peter and the Wolf, 8–7, 8–8
Rossini William Tell Overture, 6–10
Schubert Trout, The, 5–10, 5–11
Sousa Sempre Fidelis, 3–5, 3–6

SKILLS

ACCOMPANYING

Ants Go Marching, The, 12–7
Black and Gold, 2–14, 2–15
Canoe Song, 1–10
New Year's Chords, 5–2
Peanuts Peanuts Peanuts, 7–2
Pizza for All, 5–6
Sing of Peace, 1–3, 1–4
Thank You, Lord, 3–11
This Land Is Your Land, 11–3, 11–4
What Baseball's About, 11–8, 11–9
What Do We Plant When We Plant the Tree? 8–6

CHORAL READING

Little Orphant Annie, 2–10, 2–11
What Do We Plant When We Plant the Tree? 8–6

CREATING, COMPOSING, IMPROVISING

Aaron Copland Hall of Fame, 3–7
April Fool, 8–1, 8–2
Bushels of Apples, 2–1

Christopher Columbus, 2–3
Dot Dot Dot Dash, 4–3
Father's Day Song, A, 10–4
Grandmas Are Like That, 1–1
Grandpas Are Like That, 1–2
Hello, How Are You? 7–6
Hooray! Hooray! 10–5
I Love to Read, 8–4
I'm a Clown, 12–1, 12–2
Invent a Musical Instrument, 6–3
Little Orphant Annie, 2–10, 2–11
Make Your Own String Instrument, 4–6
Martin, 5–5
Names and Faces, 1–12
On the First Thanksgiving, 3–10
Paddy Works on the Railway, 7–8
Popping, Popping, 2–2
Singing Telegram, A, 11–7
Song for the New Year, A, 5–1
Sounds of Autumn, 1–7
Take Care of Your Grin, 6–1
Thank You, Teachers, 10–3

That's What Mothers Are Made Of, 9–8
Three Billy Goats Gruff, 2–6
Variations on a Familiar Carol, 4–12
Windy Days of March, 7–15
You Can't Top My Limerick, 9–10, 9–11

CONDUCTING

I'm a Clown, 12–1, 12–2
Sing and Conduct, 12–3

GAMES

Caught in a Spider Web, 2–17, 2–18, 2–19
Christmas Carol Challenge, 4–8
Counting Acorns, 1–8
Gunpowder Run, 5–12, 5–13
Love to Me, Love to You, 6–4, 6–5
Music Trivia, 5–3
Names and Faces, 1–12
Ten Little Costumes, 2–9
Who Stowed Away? 2–4, 2–5

FORM

Doo Dah Doo Dah, 5–9
Figure Eight Forms, 5–7
Fossils, 9–5
Halloween Rondo, 2–20, 2–21
Hanukkah, 4–4
Have a Picnic, 11–1
Hooray! Hooray! 10–5
Hopping From Form to Form, 10–6
Jingle Bells, 4–9, 4–10
Johnny Appleseed, 7–7
Let's Go Fly a Kite, 7–14
Little Fugue in G Minor, 7–9
Love Somebody, 6–6
Love Somebody, 6–7
Maple Leaf Rag, 3–9
Martin, 5–5
Sandwich Music, 3–3
Sempre Fidelis, 3–5
Sempre Fidelis, 3–6
Stars and Stripes Forever, The, 9–12, 9–13
Surprise Symphony, 7–12
Thank You, Teachers, 10–3
Trout, The, 5–10, 5–11
Variations on a Familiar Carol, 4–12
William Tell Overture, 6–10
You Can't Top My Limerick, 9–10, 9–11

HARMONY

Ants Go Marching, The, 12–7
Black and Gold, 2–14, 2–15
Brave Americans, 9–14
It's Raining, 8–12
New Year's Chords, 5–2

They Call It Barbershop, 8–3
This Land is Your Land, 11–3, 11–4
Trick or Treat, 2–16
Unsquare Dance, 4–1

INSTRUMENTS

Invent a Musical Instrument, 6–3
Make Your Own String Instrument, 4–6
Music of the Sitar, 12–4, 12–5
Peter and the Wolf, 8–7, 8–8
Saxophones and Their Cousins, 3–4
Violins and How They Work, 4–5
Young Person's Guide to the Orchestra, 3–8

LISTENING

Christmas Carol Challenge, 4–8
Contrasts, 5–4
Fossils, 9–5
Hallelujah Chorus, 4–11
Have a Picnic, 11–1
Hopping From Form to Form, 10–6
Jingle Bells, 4–9, 4–10
Let's Go Fly a Kite, 7–14
Little Fugue in G Minor, 7–9
Long–Eared Personages, 9–3
Maple Leaf Rag, 3–9
Minute Waltz, The, 6–8
Music of the Sitar, 12–4, 12–5
Peter and the Wolf, 8–7, 8–8
Rhapsody in Blue, 1–9
Royal March of the Lion, 9–4
Sandwich Music, 3–3
Saxophones and Their Cousins, 3–4
Sempre Fidelis, 3–5
Sempre Fidelis, 3–6
Stars and Stripes Forever, The, 9–12, 9–13
Surprise Symphony, 7–12
Swing Era, The, 7–3
Symphony No. 40, 5–8
Symphony No. Five, 4–2
Trout, The, 5–10, 5–11
Unsquare Dance, 4–1
William Tell Overture, 6–10
Young Person's Guide to the Orchestra, 3–8

MATCHING PITCHES

Counting Acorns, 1–8
Who Stowed Away? 2–4, 2–5

MELODY

Easter Egg Hunt, 8–9, 8–10
February Melodies, 6–11
Long–Eared Personages, 9–3
May Baskets, 9–1
Over the River and Through the Wood, 3–12
Royal March of the Lion, 9–4

Star Spangled Melody, A, 7–5
Symphony No. Five, 4–2
Teddy Bear, Teddy Bear, 11–6

METER

I'm a Clown, 12–1, 12–2
Sing and Conduct, 12–3

MOVEMENT

Fossils, 9–5
It's Time to Turn to Spring, 8–5
Jingle Bells, 4–9, 4–10
Johnny Appleseed, 7–7
Let's Go Fly a Kite, 7–14
Long–Eared Personages, 9–3
Raking Leaves, 1–13
Royal March of the Lion, 9–4

MUSIC THEORY

Catch a Fish, 10–1
Catch a Fly, 11–10
Caught in a Spider Web, 2–17, 2–18, 2–19
Gunpowder Run, 5–12, 5–13
Lions and Lambs, 7–13
Tennis, Anyone? 12–8

PERFORMING

Extra! Extra! Our School Is Great!, 3–1
Halloween Rondo, 2–20, 2–21
It's Time to Turn to Spring, 8–5
Johnny Appleseed, 7–7
Little Orphant Annie, 2–10, 2–11
Names and Faces, 1–12
Nutcracker, The, 4–13
O'er the Ramparts, 7–4
Peanuts Peanuts Peanuts, 7–2
Pizza for All, 5–6
Raking Leaves, 1–13
Songs from Around the World, 2–7, 2–8
Three Billy Goats Gruff, 2–6
Turkey Shoot, 3–13
What Baseball's About, 11–8, 11–9

PLAYING INSTRUMENTS

Jingle Bells, 4–9, 4–10
Love Somebody, 6–7
New Year's Chords, 5–2
Nine Lives, 2–12, 2–13
Peanuts Peanuts Peanuts, 7–2
Symphony No. Five, 4–2
Tennis, Anyone? 12–8
Thank You, Lord, 3–11
They Call It Barbershop, 8–3

This Land is Your Land, 11–3, 11–4
What Do We Plant When We Plant the Tree? 8–6
Yankee Doodle, 11–5

READING/WRITING MUSIC

A Tisket, A Tasket, 9–2
Back to School, 12–10
Brahms Lullaby, 9–9
Canoe Song, 1–11
Canoeing Fun, 12–9
Catch a Fish, 10–1
Catch a Fly, 11–10
Caught in a Spider Web, 2–17, 2–18, 2–19
Dive On In, the Water's Fine!, 10–2
Easter Egg Hunt, 8–9, 8–10
February Melodies, 6–11
Flowering Rhythms, 9–15
Give A Cheer, 1–6
Grandmas Are Like That, 1–1
Grandpas Are Like That, 1–2
Holiday Rhythms, 4–7
I'm a Clown, 12–1, 12–2
Lions and Lambs, 7–13
Love Somebody, 6–6
Love Somebody, 6–7
Lovely Rhythms, 6–10
May Baskets, 9–1
Nine Lives, 2–12, 2–13
Teddy Bear, Teddy Bear, 11–6
Tennis, Anyone? 12–8
Yankee Doodle, 11–5

RESEARCH

American Composers, 3–2
Figure Eight Forms, 5–7
Lions and Lambs, 7–13
Songs from Around the World, 2–7, 2–8
Swing Era, The, 7–3

RHYTHM

Back to School, 12–10
Canoeing Fun, 12–9
Dive On In, the Water's Fine!, 10–2
Flowering Rhythms, 9–15
Give A Cheer, 1–6
Holiday Rhythms, 4–7
Love to Me, Love to You, 6–4, 6–5
Lovely Rhythms, 6–10
Names and Faces, 1–12
Peanuts Peanuts Peanuts, 7–2
Raking Leaves, 1–13
Royal March of the Lion, 9–4
Symphony No. 40, 5–8
Ten Little Costumes, 2–9
Turkey Shoot, 3–13

Unsquare Dance, 4–1
Welcome Springtime, 8–11
What Baseball's About, 11–8, 11–9

ROUNDS

Canoe Song, 1–10
Sing of Peace, 1–3, 1–4
Thank You, Lord, 3–11

SEQUENCING

Doo Dah Doo Dah, 5–9
Hanukkah, 4–4
Star Spangled Melody, A, 7–5
Welcome Springtime, 8–11

SINGING

Ants Go Marching, The 12–7
Brahms Lullaby, 9–9
Brave Americans, 9–14
Canoe Song, 1–10

Grandmas Are Like That, 1–1
Grandpas Are Like That, 1–2
Hallelujah, 9-6, 9-7
It's Raining, 8-12
Jingle Bells, 4-9, 4-10
Johnny Appleseed, 7-7
Love Somebody, 6-7
Nine Lives, 2-12, 2-13
Over the River and Through the Wood, 3-12
Sing and Conduct, 12-3
Sing of Peace, 1-3, 1-4
Teddy Bear, Teddy Bear, 11-6
Tennis, Anyone? 12-8
Thank You, Lord, 3-11
They Call It Barbershop, 8-3
This Land Is Your Land, 11-3, 11-4
Trick or Treat, 2-16
You Can't Top My Limerick, 9-10, 9-11

TRANSPOSING

Will We Have More Winter? 6-2